W9-CYG-171

I wish to express my love and gratitude to my partner Chef Mike Trabel, for his moral support; to Kathryn Hill, my guardian angel, social media manager and Facebook co-administrator; to Jason Friedman, Facebook co-administrator and photographer extraordinaire; to The Gentle Chef Group moderators on Facebook: Martina Moore, Cheryl Wedin, Michael Rogers, Melissa Keller, and Sandra Pope Hays; and to all of our wonderful Facebook group members for their continuing support and encouragement.

This book is dedicated to you...

For questions and advice regarding the recipes
please join the Gentle Chef Group on Facebook at:
https://www.facebook.com/groups/thegentlechef

Please also visit The Gentle Chef website at:
http://thegentlechef.com

Cover photo of assorted non-dairy cheeses and fresh fruit by Skye Michael Conroy

Business contact: thegentlechef@gmail.com

Website: http://thegentlechef.com

ISBN-13: 978-1499590425

ISBN-10: 1499590423

Table of Contents

An Introduction   1

The Non-Dairy Glossary   2

Non-Dairy Milks   12

    Soymilk   12

    Quick Buttermilk   13

    Whole Soymilk and Chocolate Soymilk   14

    Raw Cashew Milk   15

    Chocolate Cashew Milk and Hot Chocolate   16

    Almond Milk   17

    Rice Milk   18

    Horchata   18

Non-Dairy Creams   19

    Crēme   19

    Quick Crème Fraîche   20

    Sweetened Coffee Creamer #1   21

    Cashew Cream   22

    Sweetened Coffee Creamer #2   23

    Chai Thai Iced Tea   24

    Heavy Whipping Crēme   25

    Organic Powdered Sugar   26

    Whipped Coconut Cream   27

Non-Dairy Butter   28

    Better Butter   28

    Seasoned Butter   29

Cultured Non-Dairy Butter, Buttermilk and Creams   30

    Rejuvelac   30

    Vital Butter   33

    Cultured Raw Buttermilk   34

    Buttermilk Ranch Dressing and Dip   35

Chilled Cucumber Buttermilk Soup   36

Cultured Sour Cream   37

Cultured Crème Fraîche   38

Greek-Style Yogurt   38

Greek Tzatziki   40

Indian Raita   41

Mango Lassi   41

An Introduction to Non-Dairy Cheeses   **42**

   Cultured Cashew-Based Cheeses   **44**

   Cream Cheese   45

   Chèvre   46

   Peppercorn Chèvre   47

   Chèvre with Fines Herbes   47

   Chèvre with Mulled Wine Swirl   48

   Chèvre with Rosemary Balsamic Swirl   49

   White Cheddar Amandine   50

   Extra-Sharp White Cheddar   51

   Bleu Cheese   52

   Chunky Bleu Cheese Dressing   53

   Iceberg Wedge Salad with Chunky Bleu Cheese Dressing   53

   Block and Wheel Cheeses   **54**

   An Introduction   54

   Preparation and Cooking Technique   57

   Troubleshooting Tips   59

   Mozzarella Fior di Latte   60

   Saganaki   61

   Eggplant Rollatini   62

   Mozzarella di Tuscano   63

   Mozzarella di Campana   64

   Mozzarella Fresco   65

Insalata Mozzarella Fresco								66

Pizza Margherita								67

Provolone Affumicata (Smoked Provolone)								68

French Brie and Camembert								69

Brie (or Camembert) en Croûte with Caramelized Mushrooms and Onions								70

Pepper Jack								71

Dill Havarti								72

Suisse								73

Muenster								74

Smoked Gouda								75

Smoked Gouda, Spinach and Artichoke Dip								76

Golden Cheddar								77

Broccoli Cheddar Soup								78

Golden Stock								79

Americana								80

Potato Cheese Soup								81

Gloucester with Onions and Chives								82

Tofu-Based Cheeses								**83**

Sharp Tofu Cheddar								83

Mediterranean Herbed Feta								85

Chèvre Soja with Basil Pesto and Sun-Dried Tomatoes								86

Basil Pesto								87

Gorgonzola								88

Gorgonzola, Pear and Candied Walnut Salad								89

Queso Fresco								90

Creamy Ricotta (with optional herbs)								91

Spinach Ricotta								91

Baked Manicotti								92

Chef's Best Marinara Sauce								93

Cottage Cheese								94

Garlic Herb Gournay 95

Zesty Onion Dill Gournay 96

Miscellaneous Cheeses **97**

Hard Parmesan 97

Garlic Parmesan Crostini 98

Risotto Parmesan 98

Grated Parmesan 99

Italian Mascarpone 100

Cheese Sauces **101**

Golden Cheddar Sauce 101

Classic Mac' and Cheese 102

Scalloped Potatoes Gratin 103

Sauce Fromage Blanc 104

Potatoes Dauphinoise 105

Mornay Sauce 106

Queso Nacho Sauce 107

Queso Blanco Sauce 108

Salsa con Queso 109

Cheese Melts **110**

Colby Melt 110

Twice-Baked Cheesy Broccoli Potatoes 111

Jarlsberg Melt 112

Käsespätzle (German Spätzle with Cheese and Onions) ... 113

Spätzle 114

Tangy Cheddar Melt 115

Classic Grilled Cheese 116

Cheesy Broccoli, Cauliflower and Rice Casserole 117

Gruyère Melt 118

Gruyère and Chive Mashed Potatoes with Peppered Walnuts ... 119

French Onion Soup 120

Brown Stock   121

Fondue   122

Non-Dairy Seasoning Blends   **123**

Instant Cheddar Cheese Sauce Mix   123

Nacho Cheese No'ritos Seasoning   124

Cool Buttermilk Ranch No'ritos Seasoning   125

Eggless Egg Specialties   **126**

Sunrise Scramble   126

Sunrise Scramble Seasoning Blend   127

Sunnyside-Ups   128

No-Yolks Sauce   129

Over-Easys   130

No-No Huevos Rancheros   131

Eggless Eggs Mornay   133

Eggless Omelets   134

Eggless Frittata   135

Mushroom, Onion and Suisse Quiche   136

Bedeviled Eggless Eggs   137

Eggless Egg Salad   139

No-Eggy Mayo   140

Non-Dairy Sweet Treats   **142**

Italian Mascarpone Cheesecake   142

Graham Cracker or Cookie Crumb Pie Shell   143

Chocolate Mascarpone Cheesecake   144

Crème Caramel   145

Fresh Fruit Gelato   146

Vanilla Bean (or Chocolate) Gelato   146

Marshmallows   147

Appendix - U.S. to Metric Conversions   **149**

Recipe Index   **150**

An Introduction

While abstaining from meat comes easy to some, abstaining from dairy foods remains the greatest obstacle for many who consider or attempt the transition to a plant-based diet. For many established vegans, commercial non-dairy foods are often not satisfying, whether due to lack of flavor or inaccurate flavor, odd texture, the inclusion of too many refined and processed ingredients, or simply lack of availability.

The Non-Dairy Evolution Cookbook is an expansion and revision of my work with non-dairy and egg-free recipes from my first two publications, The Gentle Chef Cookbook and The Non-Dairy Formulary. In this new book, I've incorporated many different and new ingredients, techniques and recipes to create non-dairy foods that are as similar to their dairy counterparts as possible. If some recipes appear repeated from my first two publications, it's because the ingredients and/or techniques have been modified or improved in some way or are essential to the other recipes. Non-dairy cuisine is still a new frontier and change is inevitable. The word "evolution" in the title of the cookbook refers not only to the shift in human consciousness towards a more compassionate way of cooking, but to my own progression in developing high-quality non-dairy recipes.

Hopefully with so many tasty new options, cravings will be satisfied and there will be no more excuses for continuing dairy and egg consumption. I think you'll be delighted with the flavors and textures that these new recipes provide; however, please keep in mind that my formulations are based upon distant memories of dairy flavors and textures. It's been many years since I've consumed dairy and egg products, so if you've recently transitioned to non-dairy foods and have a keen memory, my interpretations may not match your interpretations exactly.

Cooking is an art, but producing non-dairy foods is a science, much like the science of baking. The recipes depend upon accurate measurements and "eye-balling" measurements or making substitutions can result in poor or failed results. When and if substitutions can be made, they will be indicated.

High-powered kitchen appliances are recommended, and in some cases required, for producing the best results with some non-dairy foods, whether you are using my recipes or someone else's recipes. I realize this can be expensive, but if cooking is your passion, then good quality equipment and cooking tools should be a priority. We all prioritize our incomes by what's important to us. Good quality equipment will also save a great deal of time and frustration in the kitchen and will make cooking a pleasure rather than a chore.

You won't find nutrition information included with the recipes. That's not what this book is about. The primary goal of this book is to break the reliance on animal-based foods for ethical reasons and secondly, to provide superior alternatives to commercial non-dairy foods. Non-dairy creams, cheeses and desserts are not intended to be staples of the plant-based diet. Some of the recipes contain significant amounts of plant fats and calories. These foods are intended to be consumed in moderation as a pleasurable and satisfying addition to a well-balanced plant-based diet. The recipes were created using wholesome ingredients as much as possible and refined ingredients were included only when absolutely necessary to achieve proper textures.

My recipes are not the only way to produce these foods, nor are they necessarily the best way. They're simply my way based upon what has worked for me. Creating high quality non-dairy foods is a complex art and there is no doubt that I have many discoveries to make in the future. The recipes will continue to evolve as I continue to learn. I invite you to join me on my journey of discovery...

The Non-Dairy Glossary

Some of the ingredients and kitchen tools in this cookbook may be very familiar and others may not be familiar at all. Before attempting the recipes, it's helpful to familiarize yourself with these items and understand what they are and why they are being used.

Agar, also known as "agar agar", is a tasteless seaweed derivative and a widely used plant-based replacement for gelatin. It is used in some non-dairy cheeses, when appropriate, as a firming agent and is especially useful for creating custard-like textures in desserts.

Agar is not heat-reversible, in other words, once set it will not re-melt, at least not completely. Therefore it is not the best option for preparing cheeses when smooth melting is a desired characteristic.

Agar is also available in flake form (and occasionally stick form), but the powdered form dissolves more readily in hot water and ounce per ounce is more economical (at least this has been my experience). For this reason I recommend and use the powdered form. Agar powder can be purchased in most health food and natural food stores or mail ordered through the internet. If you only have access to the flake or stick form, the weight conversion is as follows:

1 teaspoon of agar powder = 3 g/.1 oz

Therefore for every teaspoon of agar powder required in a recipe, you would need 3 grams or .1 ounce of agar flakes or agar stick. By volume, the flake to powder conversion is roughly 4 tsp flakes to 1 tsp powder.

Arrowroot powder is a starch obtained from the rhizomes (rootstock) of several tropical plants, traditionally *Maranta arundinacea*, but also from Florida arrowroot (*Zamia pumila*). Arrowroot powder acts as a food thickening agent and can be used in equal amounts as a substitute for cornstarch or unmodified potato starch for most cooking applications; however, it has been my experience that it produces an unappetizing texture in dessert puddings and pie fillings, similar to that produced by tapioca flour. For preparing dessert puddings and pie fillings, cornstarch remains my thickening starch of choice.

Ascorbic acid is a form of vitamin C. It is a naturally occurring organic compound with antioxidant properties that is found in citrus fruits, melons and berries. Ascorbic acid is used to prevent oxidation in green vegetables helping them to maintain their color. It is also used to acidify water which helps prevent cut fruits and vegetables such as apples and potatoes from oxidizing (browning). For the purposes of this cookbook, it can be used in powdered form as a substitute for lactic acid powder when absolutely necessary (although it won't provide the same lactic dairy flavor).

Blanched almonds refer to raw almonds that have had their skins removed by brief immersion in boiling water, resulting in skinless white almonds. Stir-fries and pilafs often call for blanched almonds because the skins may separate from the almonds as the food cooks, leaving husk residues in the finished dish. However, unblanched almonds are better for snacking because the skin contributes to the toasty flavor of almonds. Almond meal is comprised of either blanched or unblanched ground almonds, while almond flour usually refers to finely ground blanched almonds. Blanched or unblanched almonds, almond meal or almond flour can all be used for preparing almond milk, with blanched almonds/meal/flour producing a milder flavor.

Carrageenan is a seaweed derivative that has been used in cooking for hundreds of years as a thickening, stabilizing and gelling agent. Carrageenan is produced in three forms: iota, kappa and lambda. Lambda carrageenan is widely used in commercial foods including many plant-based foods, such as salad dressings, veggie dogs, non-dairy milks and ice creams, just to name a few. It is also the form of carrageenan that has been the subject of a great deal of media hype for its alleged gastrointestinal effects.

Kappa carrageenan, which is molecularly different from lambda carrageenan, is used as a firming agent for the Block and Wheel Cheeses in this cookbook. Iota carrageenan, which is also molecularly different from lambda carrageenan, is used to replace gelatin in the marshmallow recipe in this cookbook. Kappa and iota carrageenan are not available in health or natural food stores but are available online through specialty food ingredient retailers such as Modernist Pantry. Modernist Pantry offers affordable and superior quality kappa carrageenan in a home size (50 grams), for those who wish to experiment with cheese making, and a professional size (400 grams) for those who prepare the Block and Wheel Cheeses on a regular basis. The iota carrageenan is also sold in the home size (50 grams) which is sufficient for occasional marshmallow making.

Modernist Pantry also ships worldwide and is an excellent resource for obtaining superior quality lactic acid powder, agar powder, soy lecithin powder, Versawhip 600K, perfected guar gum, xanthan gum and sodium alginate. Please visit the Modernist Pantry website at: *www.modernistpantry.com*

Kappa carrageenan is harvested from various locations around the world and refined according to different standards by each manufacturer; therefore, the quality of carrageenan purchased from other sources cannot be guaranteed. **Kappa carrageenan produced by Molecule-R™ is not compatible with the cheese formulas in this cookbook and may not perform as expected.**

Cheesecloth is a woven gauze-like cotton cloth used primarily in cheese making. In non-dairy applications, it can be used in place of a nut milk bag for straining solids from plant milks. It can also be used for squeezing water from block tofu to sufficiently dry the tofu for use in various recipes. Cheesecloth is not as finely woven as nylon nut milk bags, so 4 layers will be needed for efficient straining of plant milks.

Citric acid powder is a white crystalline powder used to add acidity, or a sour taste, to foods. It is an organic acid and acts as a natural preservative. Citric acid exists naturally in a variety of fruits and vegetables, most notably citrus fruits like lemons and limes. Interestingly, citric acid is used as the main ripening agent in the first steps of making dairy mozzarella cheese. Citric acid powder can be used as a substitute for lactic acid powder if necessary (although it won't provide the same lactic dairy flavor).

Cornstarch is a familiar food thickening agent. However, in the United States it is almost always derived from genetically-modified corn. Purchase non-GMO cornstarch whenever possible or substitute with equal amounts of unmodified potato starch or arrowroot powder. For preparing dessert puddings and pie fillings, non-GMO cornstarch remains my thickening starch of choice.

Emulsion refers to a mixture of two or more liquids that are normally immiscible (non-mixable or un-blendable) and emulsification refers to the process in which two or more liquids which are normally immiscible are blended together to create an emulsion. During this process, larger fat globules are broken down into smaller, evenly distributed particles.

Examples of emulsions in this cookbook include Better Butter and Vital Butter, soy-based Crèmes, No-Eggy Mayo, No-Yolks Sauce, Cheese Melts, Cheese Sauces, and the Block and Wheel Cheeses. Some emulsions are naturally stable, such as soymilk. However, most emulsions are inherently unstable, do not form spontaneously and require some form of kinetic action, such as shaking or stirring, to combine them together. Over time, unstable emulsions tend to revert back to their original separate components, unless an emulsifier is added to hold them together. An emulsifier (also known as an "emulgent") is a substance, such as mustard in mayonnaise and lecithin in non-dairy butter, that stabilizes an emulsion and helps hold the components together. Kappa carrageenan, although technically a gelling agent and not an emulsifier, serves to stabilize and hold the plant milk and oil emulsion together when preparing the Block and Wheel Cheeses.

Why do emulsions break? If the temperature is too high when cooking the Block and Wheel Cheeses, for example, or the oil is added too quickly when making mayonnaise, then the mixture can lose its ability to hold together. When this happens, the emulsification has "broken". If the mixture begins to look grainy, or the oil is beginning to separate from the mixture, then this is a good indication that the emulsion is about to break. For the Block and Wheel Cheeses, removing the mixture from the heat source and stirring vigorously will usually remedy the problem. Regrettably with egg-free mayonnaise, you will need to discard the mixture and start over. Egg yolk is a classic remedy for "broken" mayonnaise, but we don't use eggs; however, you could try rescuing the mayonnaise by adding a teaspoon of soy lecithin powder and blitzing the mixture with an immersion blender (since lecithin is the emulsifying component in egg yolk).

Filtered or spring water is water that has either been purified through some form of filtration to remove chlorine and impurities or sourced and bottled from underground aquifers or pure mountain streams. Pure water is essential for producing live bacterial cultures which are used for fermenting cashew-based milk, cream and cheese; however, filtered or spring water is recommended in all recipes whether they are cultured or uncultured. Tap water filters, such as PUR™ and Brita™ are very economical and will filter large amounts of tap water effectively and conveniently.

Food processors are similar to blenders in many ways. The primary difference is that food processors use interchangeable blades and disks (attachments) instead of a fixed blade. Also, their bowls are wider and shorter, a more appropriate shape for processing solid or semi-solid foods. Usually, little or no liquid is required in the operation of the food processor, unlike a blender, which requires some amount of liquid to move the particles around the blade. However, while food processors have several advantages over blenders, they will not produce the ultra-smooth textures that high-powered blenders can achieve.

Fruit acids refer specifically to raw apple cider vinegar, citrus juices and wine vinegars (other vinegars, such as rice vinegar, are made from rice and distilled white vinegar is made from malt or corn). Raw apple cider vinegar and lemon juice are used either alone or in combination to increase acidity, add tanginess and/or mimic the flavor of lactic acid in uncultured non-dairy foods. Fruit acids also increase acidity and enhance flavor in a wide variety of cuisine. If a recipe calls for fresh lemon juice, avoid commercial juice sold in plastic "lemon" containers if possible, as lemon oil is often added as a flavoring and this may adversely affect the flavor of the finished dish. As a general rule, fresh is always best and this applies to most ingredients used in cooking.

GMO (genetically modified organism) refers to agricultural products that are genetically altered for higher yields and insect and disease resistance. There have been no long-term studies proving the safety or danger towards human health from these modifications. Corn and soybeans are the most commonly modified, so purchase organic whenever possible. Many health-oriented and organic food companies will state "non-GMO" directly on their labels.

Guar gum, also called *guaran*, is a natural substance derived from the ground seeds of the guar plant which grows primarily in Pakistan and the northern regions of India. Food gums, such as guar, belong to a group of stabilizing compounds called *polysaccharides*. It is used as a thickener and stabilizer in making non-dairy butter; it adds viscosity and stretch to cheese melts; and it prevents ice crystallization in ice cream. Without guar gum as a stabilizer, non-dairy ice cream would become coarse, icy and hard due to the growth of ice crystals as the mixture freezes. Guar gum can be purchased in some supermarkets, in most health food and natural food stores, or purchased online through food retail websites such as ModernistPantry.com and Amazon.com. Guar gum can be replaced with an equal amount of sodium alginate or xanthan gum if desired.

High-powered blenders, such as the Vitamix® or Blendtec®, are required for processing cashews and other thick ingredients such as tofu. Standard blenders simply don't have the power to churn through the ingredients used to make cheeses and you will quickly burn out the motor.

A bonus feature of the Vitamix™ blenders is the "tamper tool" which can be inserted through the lid. This helps keep thick mixtures turning in the blades, without having to start and stop the blender as frequently to stir.

However, one drawback to the high-powered blenders is their exorbitant price, but as the old saying goes, "you get what you pay for". They're definitely worth the investment and will save you countless hours of time and frustration in the kitchen. I have heard that the Ninja® blender and Oster® Versa blender are affordable and effective alternatives; however, I haven't had the opportunity to work with these appliances.

Immersion blenders, or stick blenders, are kitchen appliances that blend ingredients or purée food in the container in which they are being prepared. Immersion blenders are distinguished from standard/high-powered blenders and food processors as the latter two require that the food be placed in a special container for processing. They are also distinguished from hand mixers which do not chop the food as it is blended.

Kala namak, also known as Himalayan black salt, is an Indian salt with a high mineral content, most notably sulfur, which gives it its characteristic and pungent "hard-boiled egg" smell. Oddly enough, it is pink in color when dry but turns black when moistened. It is used in eggless egg foods as it imparts a cooked egg flavor and aroma. Be advised, that if you detest the sulfurous odor of hard-boiled eggs, you probably will not care for this salt. Kala namak is considered a cooling spice in Ayurvedic medicine and is used as a digestive aid. It can be found in specialty food stores as well as though the internet. Himalayan pink salt is not the same thing, so this can make purchasing rather confusing since kala namak is also pink when dry. Specifically look for the names *kala namak* or *Himalayan black salt*.

Lactic Acid Powder is used as an alternative to lemon juice for adding flavor, acidity and tanginess to non-dairy foods. Lactic acid is sometimes referred to as "milk acid", since lactic acid is the compound responsible for causing milk to sour and since it was first isolated in a laboratory from sour milk in 1780. Lactic acid is a by-product of the fermentation of sugar by the lactobacillus bacteria.

Commercial lactic acid powder is almost always produced by the fermentation of carbohydrates from plants (rather than being derived from milk), but always double-check your source before purchasing. It has advantages over lemon juice in many non-dairy applications since it is the precise flavor produced in cultured foods, whereas lemon juice (which contains citric and ascorbic acids) can only mimic the flavor of lactic acid produced during culturing. Another advantage is that it increases acidity without adding additional moisture or liquid volume and this works well in non-dairy cheeses when a drier, firmer texture is desired. In uncultured non-dairy food applications, commercial lactic acid is often paired with vinegar because lactic acid only provides one flavor component of actual bacterial culturing.

ModernistPantry.com is my recommended source for obtaining this relatively inexpensive ingredient. Modernist Pantry has assured me that their lactic acid is derived solely from plant sources, specifically sugar cane and beets. Exercise caution when purchasing lactic acid in liquid form. Liquid lactic acid is commonly used as a pH buffer for home brewing beer. Unless its source is indicated, it may be derived from dairy. The liquid form would also increase liquid volume or moisture content in recipes, which is undesirable when creating firmer, drier cheese textures. That's the whole point of using the dry form. Citric acid powder or ascorbic acid powder (Vitamin C) can be used as a substitute for lactic acid powder but will not provide the precise flavor.

Lecithin, simply stated, is a natural, waxy substance derived from the processing of organic soybeans. It is an essential ingredient for promoting the emulsification of soymilk or nut milk with oil when making non-dairy butter; in other words, it binds the oil and milk together. Organic soy lecithin can be purchased in liquid, powder or granular forms and can be found in most health food and natural food stores, or online through food retail websites. Granular lecithin does not dissolve well in the butter formulas, so I highly recommend grinding it into a fine powder before using.

For those who are allergic to soy, sunflower lecithin, which is derived from sunflower seeds, can be substituted for soy lecithin. However, it does not possess the rich golden color of soy lecithin. In fact, liquid sunflower lecithin has the color of melted chocolate while the dry version has a soft beige tint, so expect a color variation in the butter when using sunflower lecithin. Unless you have an allergy to soy, I highly recommend the soy lecithin over the sunflower lecithin.

In my experience, liquid soy or sunflower lecithin produces better results over their dry counterparts; however, the liquid form is very sticky and can be rather difficult to remove from measuring utensils and blending tools. Coat the inside of the measuring spoon with a small amount of the melted coconut oil or vegetable oil before measuring to reduce adhesion to the spoon. Wipe the spoon with a paper towel to remove the excess residue and then wash with hot, soapy water by hand or in an automatic dishwasher. The immersion blender or food processor, and any other utensils used to make butter, will also need to be thoroughly washed in this manner as well. If cleanup is an issue, consider using the dry lecithin powder or the granules ground into powder form.

The conversion ratio for lecithin in the non-dairy butter recipes is as follows:

4 tsp/20 ml liquid lecithin

=

2 T plus 2 tsp/.8 oz/24 g dry lecithin powder

=

.8 oz/24 g dry lecithin granules

Mise en place (pronounced *meez-ahn-plahs*) is a French term literally translated as "put in place". Mise en place refers to assembly of all ingredients and tools and measurement of all ingredients before cooking begins. It is an important culinary technique and one of the most often neglected. Many people scramble for supplies and tools and measure ingredients while cooking. This is a bad habit that often leads to mistakes and failures. Practice *mise en place* consistently and your cooking experience will be both a pleasure and success.

Mellow White Miso Paste is a Japanese seasoning paste produced by the fermentation of soybeans (or chickpeas or barley) with salt and the fungus *kōjikin (aspergillis oryzae)*. Miso adds *umami*, a Japanese word used to describe a pleasant savory flavor. Mellow white miso paste is used as a culturing and flavoring ingredient in many non-dairy cheeses, as it contributes to a "ripened" cheese flavor.

Mellow white miso paste can be found in natural food markets and health food stores in the refrigerator section. It has a very long refrigerator shelf life, usually about 2 years. If you're new to miso, be aware that mellow white miso is actually beige or light brown in color and not actually white. If you're allergic to soy, look for varieties made from chickpeas or barley.

Mustard in dry, ground powder form is a bitter and pungent flavoring spice. In the non-dairy cheeses in this cookbook, it imparts degrees of pungency. In the No-Eggy Mayo recipe it serves a dual purpose as a flavoring ingredient and an emulsifier. The coating of the mustard seed contains a fair amount of mucilage (a thick, sticky substance) which helps to coat molecules of oil, allowing them to coexist harmoniously with watery substances. This helps the oil and soymilk bind together which helps stabilize the mayonnaise. For this reason, do not omit the mustard powder in the mayonnaise formula.

Nut milk bags are made from ultra-fine nylon mesh. They are very effective for straining micro-fine solids from nut, seed and grain milks and for straining the okara (pulp) from soymilk. They are also economical as they can be washed and reused repeatedly (as opposed to cheesecloth). If you cannot locate a nut milk bag, try improvising with a ladies' knee-high nylon stocking.

To use the bag, first wash your hands thoroughly. Hold the bag at the top and place it over a large container. Pour in the milk or cream and with your other hand gently massage and squeeze the bag to press the liquid through the mesh. Turn the bag inside out to rinse and discard or compost the solids. Wash with unscented natural dish soap in hot water, rinse well and lay flat on a clean dish towel to dry.

A strainer lined with 4-layers of cheesecloth will work in a similar manner, except the milk or cream will need to be stirred with a spoon to help the liquid pass though the cheesecloth. Nut milk bags can sometimes be found in health food or natural food stores but can easily be found and purchased through the internet.

Nutritional yeast flakes are a non-active form of yeast and a source of complete protein and vitamins, especially the B-complex vitamins. It is naturally low in fat and sodium and is free of sugar and dairy. Some brands of nutritional yeast flakes, though not all, are fortified with vitamin B12. The vitamin B12 is produced separately and then added to the yeast. Nutritional yeast flakes can be found in most health and natural food stores or online through food retail websites such as Amazon.com. Bob's Red Mill™ produces superior quality, vitamin-fortified nutritional yeast flakes with a rich golden color. The conversion ratio for nutritional yeast flakes to powder is 2:1. In other words, if a recipe calls for 2 tablespoons nutritional yeast flakes, use 1 tablespoon nutritional yeast powder. Do not confuse nutritional yeast with brewer's yeast. Regrettably there is no substitute for nutritional yeast in the cheese formulas for those who cannot tolerate the flavor.

Organic is a term used to describe agricultural farming practices as well as food production, although the "organic" standard is defined differently in different regions. In general, organic farming integrates biological and mechanical practices that encourages cycling of resources, promotes ecological balance, and conserves biodiversity in crop production. Synthetic pesticides and chemical fertilizers are generally not allowed, although non-synthetic and organically approved pesticides may be used under limited conditions.

In general, organic foods are not processed using irradiation, industrial solvents, or chemical food additives. Currently, the European Union, the United States, Canada, Japan and many other countries require producers to obtain special certification based on government-defined standards in order to market food as organic within their borders. If non-organic ingredients are present, at least a certain percentage of the food's total ingredients must be organic (95% in the United States, Canada, and Australia).

Organic refined coconut oil provides the solid fat essential for thickening many of the non-dairy products in this book. In many respects, it shares striking similarities to dairy butterfat, but without the cholesterol (and animal exploitation). Coconut oil becomes semi-solid at room temperature and very solid when chilled; therefore, it must be melted for proper measurement in recipes. This can be done by removing the metal lid from the jar and placing the jar into a microwave to heat for 30 seconds to 1 minute (depending upon the solidity of the coconut oil). Avoid overheating the oil, especially when preparing cultured foods. Alternately, the jar can be placed in about an inch of simmering water and melted in the same manner. Repeated melting and re-hardening of the oil will not harm it.

The amount of coconut oil used in the recipes has been carefully calculated to produce the best results. Although it may be tempting to reduce or eliminate the oil for health and weight control purposes, this is not recommended. The non-dairy products will not thicken or set properly and this will adversely affect the finished texture. It is much better to moderate your consumption of non-dairy foods than to tamper with fat ratios in the recipes.

The best creams and cheeses, whether dairy or non-dairy, must contain fat for flavor and texture. If you've ever had low-fat dairy cheese in the past, you'll know exactly what I mean: it's dry, flavorless and does not melt well. Dairy cheese contains between 30% to 45% butterfat for low-fat varieties and upwards of 50% for regular varieties (in some cases as high as 80%). The non-dairy cheeses in this book, on average, contain between 25% to 33% plant fat. So, compared to dairy cheese, they remain well within or below the low-fat range.

Virgin organic coconut oil is not recommended for making non-dairy foods except for ice cream and other desserts. While in most cases I would always recommend less refined or less processed ingredients, this is not the case when it comes to coconut oil used in most non-dairy foods - unless you're content with your butter, creams and cheeses having a distinct coconut undertaste. Refining removes the coconut flavor and aroma from coconut oil and therefore is a better option. Save the virgin coconut oil for sweets and treats.

De-scented organic cocoa butter has properties similar to coconut oil and could potentially be used as a replacement (which would be a good option for those allergic to coconuts). However, it is not available to me locally and is very expensive through the internet; therefore I haven't had the opportunity to experiment with it at this time. Sustainably-sourced palm oil is another potential alternative but I have never worked with it.

Organic refined coconut oil can be found in many larger supermarket chains, health food stores and natural food stores or purchased online through food retail websites.

Organic sugar is made from organic sugar cane and should not be confused with refined white sugar. The juice is pressed from organic raw sugar cane, evaporated and then crushed into crystals. In adherence with strict Organic Standards, the fields are green cut and not burned or treated with herbicides or synthetic fertilizers. No chemicals or animal by-products are used to decolorize the sugar. This makes it very different from refined white sugar, which has been decolorized by filtering through animal bone char. Organic sugar is my sweetener of choice for cooking because of its availability, affordability and neutral flavor.

Pure soymilk refers to homemade or commercial soymilk that is prepared from only organic, non-GMO soybeans and water. It contains no sweeteners or thickening additives which are commonly found in most commercial brands of soymilk (and all other commercial non-dairy milks). Pure soymilk is recommended for preparing many of the non-dairy recipes in this cookbook, due to its natural stability, similarity to dairy milk in composition, and lack of additives that can interfere with emulsification and the finished texture of non-dairy foods (vitamin and calcium fortified commercial soymilk is acceptable as long as no other additives are present).

Raw Apple Cider Vinegar is a vinegar produced from organic and unpasteurized apple cider. The "mother" is made up of the yeasts and fermentation by-products that are produced when the cider ferments to vinegar. These by-products settle as sediment at the bottom of the bottle, therefore the bottle should be shaken before use. Most commercial companies pasteurize their vinegar and filter out this sediment.

Rejuvelac is a non-alcoholic fermented liquid made from grain. In this book, it serves as a culturing agent for fermenting cashew milk and cashew cream, which in turn is used for producing the finest cultured non-dairy buttermilk, sour cream and cashew-based cheeses. Lactic acid is the by-product of fermentation with rejuvelac and this acid is what creates the sour, tangy or "sharp" flavor in cultured non-dairy foods. In cheeses, this flavor intensifies and develops secondary flavor characteristics during "ripening".

Cultured non-dairy foods are a health benefit to those adhering to a plant-based diet, which can be lacking in cultured foods. These "friendly" bacteria help contribute to a healthy intestinal flora, which keeps harmful pathogens in check and also assists in the absorption of nutrients.

Note: Although kombucha contains symbiotic colonies of bacteria and yeast, they are entirely different than the lactic bacterial cultures present in rejuvelac. Kombucha cultures produce acetic acid, or vinegar, which accounts for its flavor. Therefore, kombucha cannot be used as a substitute for rejuvelac for culturing the cheeses in this cookbook. In the same manner, rejuvelac does not work for culturing yogurt, because certain strains of bacteria are required. Just because something contains a live culture, does not mean it will work in all culturing applications.

Shelf life is the length of time that a food may be stored without becoming unfit for use or consumption. However, shelf life alone is not an accurate indicator of how long a food can safely be stored. Many foods can remain fresh for several days past their recommended shelf life if stored and refrigerated properly. In contrast, if these foods have already been contaminated with harmful bacteria, the guideline becomes irrelevant. Shelf life also depends on the degradation mechanism of a specific food. Most foods can be influenced by several factors such as acid and salt content; exposure to light, heat and moisture; transmission of gases; and contamination by micro-organisms.

The general guideline for refrigerator shelf life of any prepared food that does not contain preservatives, heavy salt content or vinegar is 7 to 10 days.

Non-dairy butter will stay fresh in the refrigerator for several weeks and can be stored in the freezer for up to 3 months. Fresh almond milk, cashew milk and cashew cream has a brief refrigerator shelf life of only 4 to 5 days. However, fresh soymilk and soy-based Crēme can be refrigerated for up to 10 days. Non-dairy milks can be frozen for up to 1 month. The refrigerator shelf life for cultured cashew milk and creams is about 2 weeks.

Non-cultured cheeses have a refrigerator shelf life of 2 to 3 weeks; although vacuum-sealing the cheeses will extend their shelf life considerably. The cheeses can also be frozen for up to 3 months, although freezing may alter their texture. The refrigerator shelf life for cultured cheeses is 3 to 6 weeks, depending upon the cheese. In general, the firmer the cheese, or the lower the moisture content, the longer the shelf life.

Eggless egg foods (including mayonnaise) and prepared desserts (other than ice cream, of course) have a refrigerator shelf life of 7 to 10 days.

However, there are no hard and fast rules and these are only rough guidelines. My best advice is to use your own judgment. Obviously, if something is moldy, smells "off" or tastes odd, then it's time to discard.

Sodium alginate is a flavorless food gum derived from brown seaweed. It is used in the food industry to add viscosity and stability to a wide range of food products. In molecular gastronomy, it is combined with calcium lactate or similar compounds to create spheres of liquid surrounded by a thin jelly membrane. Sodium alginate is both food and skin safe and can be used as an alternate to guar gum and xanthan gum in this cookbook. Sodium alginate can be purchased from ModernistPantry.com.

Soymilk is a stable emulsion prepared from cooked soybeans and water ("stable" means that it does not separate like other plant milks). Soymilk contains about the same proportion of complete protein (3.5%), carbohydrates (2.9%) and fat (2%) as low-fat cow's milk. Soymilk emulsifies with plant oils better than unstable non-dairy milks. It also curdles like dairy milk in the presence of acids, which aids thickening in many non-dairy applications. There are some individuals who are allergic or sensitive to soy, although true soy allergies are much less common than allergies to nuts. If you're avoiding soy because you read somewhere that it is bad for you, please do more thorough research.

Within the context of this cookbook, pure soymilk refers to homemade or commercial soymilk that is prepared using only organic, non-GMO soybeans and water. It contains no sweeteners or thickening additives which are commonly found in many commercial brands of soymilk (and all other commercial non-dairy milks).

Pure soymilk is recommended for preparing many of the non-dairy recipes in this cookbook, due to its natural stability, similarity to dairy milk in protein/carbohydrate/fat ratios, and lack of additives that can interfere with emulsification and the finished texture of non-dairy foods (vitamin and calcium fortified commercial soymilk is acceptable as long as no other additives are present). Westsoy™ in the United States produces a pure soymilk. Homemade Soymilk (pg. 12) is an option for those who wish to prepare their own soymilk or if pure commercial soymilk is unavailable.

Many aspects of cooking are based upon food chemistry and the way ingredients interact with one another on a molecular level. There are a wide variety of plant milks available, but just because they're all labeled as "milk", does not mean they will all work in recipes in the same manner. Keep this in mind when attempting to make substitutions for soymilk in recipes unless alternative options are provided.

Soymilk Powder (instant, non-GMO) is a convenient powder for making instant soymilk. It's also an essential ingredient for Buttermilk Ranch No'ritos Seasoning (pg. 125).

Tapioca flour, also known as tapioca starch, is a carbohydrate extracted from the cassava plant (*Manihot esculenta*). It is used worldwide as a thickening agent in foods. It differs from wheat flour, rice flour, potato starch, cornstarch, and arrowroot powder in that it produces a gooey, stretchy texture when heated in liquids. This characteristic makes it an ideal thickener for non-dairy cheeses, cheese melts, cheese sauces and fondue. Tapioca flour can be purchased in some supermarkets, in most health food and natural food stores, or online through food retail websites such as Amazon.com. If you absolutely cannot obtain tapioca flour, use arrowroot powder as a substitute (although the finished texture will be different).

Tofu, or bean curd, is made from soymilk that has been coagulated and pressed into soft white blocks. It is of Chinese origin, and is also a part of East Asian and Southeast Asian cuisine such as Chinese, Japanese, Korean, Indonesian, Vietnamese, and others.

Tofu is considered a staple in plant-based diets, because of its high protein content, low content of calories and fat, high calcium and iron content and the ability to substitute for eggs in a variety of recipes. Tofu has a subtle flavor and can be used in both savory recipes and desserts.

Calcium sulfate (gypsum) is the traditional and most widely used coagulant to produce water-packed block tofu. The resulting tofu curd is tender yet firm in texture and the coagulant itself has no perceivable taste. Use of this coagulant also produces a tofu that is rich in calcium. The coagulant and soymilk are mixed together in large vats, allowed to curdle and the resulting curds are drained, pressed into blocks and then packaged.

Water-packed block tofu is sold in plastic tub containers completely immersed in water to maintain its moisture content and it will always be found in the refrigerated section of the market. It ranges in density and texture from soft to extra-firm. Soft to medium water-packed block tofu works well in eggless egg scrambles. Firm and extra-firm water-packed block tofu can be used as meat alternative; and extra-firm water-packed block tofu is used for making tofu-based cheeses. It is essential to know the difference, as the type of tofu used will definitely affect your recipe results.

Silken tofu, because of its delicate texture and neutral flavor, is used in this cookbook for a variety of cooked eggless egg foods such as Sunnyside-Ups, Over-Easys, omelets, frittatas and quiches. It's also used as an egg replacement in desserts, since it has a smoother and more custard-like texture compared to the firmer, water-packed block tofu. Magnesium chloride and calcium chloride are the coagulants (called *nigari* in Japan) used to make silken tofu. These coagulants are added to soymilk and the mixture is then sealed in 12.3 oz. aseptic cartons. In other words, the resulting bean curd is produced inside its own package, rather than being drained and pressed into blocks.

Silken tofu packaged in this manner needs no refrigeration until the carton is opened. This gives it an extended shelf life, compared to fresh water-packed tofu sold in tub containers. However, silken tofu can now also be found in 1 lb tub containers in the refrigerated section next to the firmer water-packed block tofu. This can be somewhat confusing if you're new to tofu, so it's important to read labels and be aware of what you're purchasing.

Recipes requiring extra-firm silken tofu are referring to the unrefrigerated Mori-Nu™ silken tofu (or similar) packaged in the 12.3 oz. aseptic carton. If you purchase silken tofu in a 1 lb refrigerated tub container, you will need to weigh the tofu before using in the recipe.

Tomato paste is an ingredient used in varying amounts to add a warm golden color to cheeses, melts and sauces. Look for tube tomato paste in the pasta sauce, gourmet section or spice section of your market (it's packaged like a tube of toothpaste). It stays fresh in the refrigerator much longer than canned tomato paste (which needs to be transferred to a small storage container after the can has been opened).

Tomato Powder is prepared from dehydrated, vine-ripe tomatoes and is used as an alternative to tomato paste for adding a warm golden color to cheddar-style cheeses, melts and sauces. It has advantages over tomato paste as it doesn't add additional moisture to the cheeses and is very convenient and more economical too. It can also be used in other culinary applications for enriching the tomato flavor and color of sauces, soups and stews. Look for non-GMO and preservative-free tomato powder which can be purchased in specialty food stores and through the internet (e.g., Amazon.com). For cooking purposes, use half the measured amount as you would for tomato paste.

Unmodified potato starch is one of the less familiar starches used as a food thickener. It can be used in equal amounts as an alternate to cornstarch or arrowroot powder. Unmodified potato starch works flawlessly in the eggless egg recipes and works well as a substitute for cornstarch in dessert puddings and pie fillings. Do not confuse unmodified potato starch with potato flour, which is actually ground dehydrated potatoes and avoid modified potato starch (which has been physically, enzymatically, or chemically treated in such a manner that changes its properties). Bob's Red Mill™ produces a high-quality and inexpensive unmodified potato starch.

Vegetable oil refers to any plant oil with a mild taste such as safflower, sunflower, grapeseed, canola or soybean oil. This should not be confused with commercial labeling, where "vegetable oil" usually refers to soybean oil. Olive oil, although refined and milder in flavor than virgin olive oil, is not as mild in flavor as these other oils. The best vegetable oils for high temperature cooking are safflower, sunflower, canola, peanut, and soy.

Versawhip 600K is a modified (enzyme-treated) soy protein. It is used to replace egg whites in plant-based sugar confections such as marshmallows. Versawhip 600K can be purchased from Modernist Pantry at *www.modernistpantry.com*.

Whole Raw Cashews are obtained from the fruit of the cashew tree, which is indigenous to Brazil and is now grown in other tropical climates. Although considered a nut in the culinary sense, in the botanical sense the cashew is actually a seed. Some people are allergic to cashews, but cashews are a less frequent allergen than other nuts or peanuts.

Cashews, unlike other oily tree nuts, contain up 10% of their weight in starch. When blended into a cream, this makes them more effective than other nuts for thickening water-based dishes such as soups, stews, curries and some desserts. This starch (which is comprised of a chain of glucose units) also makes cashews a more effective medium for culturing than other nuts, which in turn makes them ideal for creating the finest cultured buttermilk, creams, Greek-style yogurt and cheeses.

Whole raw cashews are also ideal for making milk for drinking purposes because of their perfect balance of sweetness and mild flavor. If possible, avoid purchasing cashew halves and pieces because they are often stale and dried out (lacking in natural moisture or oils).

Soaking the cashews in water for a minimum of 8 hours to soften them before processing is required when preparing foods with low water content, such as thick creams, cheeses and desserts. However, pre-soaking is unnecessary when larger amounts of water are used for processing (cashew milk, for example). Whole raw cashews can be expensive but are definitely more affordable when purchased in bulk.

Non-Dairy Milks

Soymilk

Soymilk is a beverage made from soybeans. It is produced by soaking dry soybeans, cooking them in water, processing them in a blender with fresh water and then straining out the solid pulp which is called *okara*. For drinking purposes, a natural sweetener can be added to suit your taste. Purchase organic, non-GMO soybeans whenever possible (we don't want to support Monsanto). "Laura" soybeans are a specific variety of soybeans that are said to produce a mild soymilk.

This recipe will yield as many quarts of soymilk as you desire. The soybeans can also be cooked ahead of time in bulk, frozen and then conveniently used as needed for making fresh soymilk. Soymilk has a refrigerator shelf life of up to 10 days.

Ingredients:

- ½ cup dry organic non-GMO soybeans for each quart of soymilk, or
  1 and ¼ cup (7.5 oz by weight) cooked soybeans for each quart of soymilk
- 3 and ½ cup water for each quart of soymilk
- ¼ tsp fine sea salt or kosher salt for each quart of soymilk

You will also need a blender for processing and a nylon nut milk bag to strain the *okara* (pulp) from the milk. A strainer lined with 4-layers of cheesecloth and a large spoon can be used in place of the nut milk bag.

Technique:

Rinse the beans to make sure they are clean and then place them into a mason jar (home canning jar) or other sealable container and fill the container with plenty of cold water to cover. Refrigerate for a minimum of 6 hours, with 12 hours being ideal. After soaking, drain the water from the beans and pour them into a large cooking pot. Add plenty of fresh water to cover the soybeans.

Bring the pot of soybeans and water to a rapid boil. Reduce the heat to a soft boil and set a timer for 30 minutes.

After cooking, drain the soybeans in a strainer or colander. Place the cooking pot into the sink, add the soybeans and fill the pot with cold water. Vigorously stir the soybeans in the water. This will help loosen some of the soybean skins. Removing the skins will reduce the amount of oligosaccharides in the finished soymilk. Oligosaccharides are starch compounds responsible for causing excessive intestinal gas whenever beans are consumed, since the human GI tract cannot break down the compounds completely.

After stirring, the soybeans will sink to the bottom of the pot while the loosened skins will float towards the top. Alternately, the soybeans can be rubbed between the palms of your hands to loosen the skins while submerged in the water.

Pour off the water into the sink, which in turn will carry most of the loosened skins with it. It's not essential to remove all the skins, just the excess. Now transfer the soybeans back to the strainer or colander to drain completely.

Next, the beans will need to be processed in a blender with fresh water. It is recommended to process and strain each quart individually. Place 1 and ¼ cup (7.5 oz by weight) cooked soybeans into a blender (if using pre-cooked frozen soybeans, be sure to thaw them first). Add 3 and ½ cup of fresh water and the salt and process the contents on high speed for 2 full minutes.

The soymilk will now need to be strained to remove the okara. To do this, wash your hands thoroughly and pour the soymilk into the nut milk bag over a large container.

While holding the top of the bag with one hand, firmly knead and squeeze the bag with your other hand to help the milk pass through the fine mesh and to extract as much of the milk as you can from the okara. This may take a few minutes, so be patient.

Optionally, place a strainer lined with 4-layers of cheesecloth over a large container and pour the milk (in increments) into the strainer. Stir the milk with a large spoon to help it pass through the cheesecloth.

Discard or compost the okara in the bag or cheesecloth or save for other uses as desired.

Transfer the milk to a sealable container and refrigerate until chilled. Initially, the bean aroma of the milk may be distinct but will diminish after chilling.

Quick Buttermilk

This quick and easy-to-make buttermilk has a tangy, refreshing flavor. Soymilk is essential for this formula since it thickens in the presence of lactic acid, which adds body to the buttermilk. It's excellent for making buttermilk pancakes, biscuits, cornbread, or for any baking purpose. It's superb for salad dressings and dips too. This recipe yields 2 cups of buttermilk. For 1 quart, simply double the recipe measurements.

Ingredients:

- 2 cups pure soymilk
- 1 tsp lactic acid powder (sorry, no substitutes for this recipe)
- ¼ tsp fine sea salt or kosher salt

Technique:

Add the ingredients to a sealable container. Shake well and refrigerate until chilled before using. Quick buttermilk has a shelf life of up to 2 weeks.

Whole Soymilk
and Chocolate Soymilk

Plain soymilk is comparable to low-fat dairy milk at about 2% fat. Whole soymilk is comparable to whole dairy milk at about 4% fat. This added richness makes whole soymilk ideal for pouring over cold cereals and for preparing deliciously creamy chocolate milk. Whole soymilk foams nicely when steamed for caffè lattes too.

The soymilk should be at or near room temperature for proper homogenization. Freshly prepared soymilk or an unchilled and unopened carton of commercial soymilk is ideal. If the soymilk is chilled, simply let it sit out at room temperature for about an hour. This recipe yields 1 quart. Whole soymilk has a refrigerator shelf life of up to 10 days.

Ingredients for whole soymilk:

- 1 quart (4 cups) pure soymilk, room temperature
- 4 tsp organic **refined** coconut oil

Additional ingredients for chocolate whole soymilk:

- ⅔ cup organic sugar, or more to taste
- ⅓ cup cocoa powder or carob powder
- 1 tsp real vanilla extract
- ¼ tsp fine sea salt or kosher salt

Technique:

Remove the metal lid and place the jar in a microwave. Heat just until the solid oil liquefies, about 30 seconds to 1 minute (this will depend upon the solidity of the coconut oil). Alternately, place the jar in about an inch of simmering water and melt the oil in the same manner. Measure 4 teaspoons and set aside.

Add the soymilk to a blender (with the additional ingredients if applicable), cover and begin processing on high speed. Drizzle the coconut oil into the milk through the opening in the blender jar's lid. Continue to process for 10 seconds after the oil has been incorporated to ensure homogenization.

Transfer the milk to a sealable container and refrigerate until chilled. Shake well before using.

Raw Cashew Milk

Many varieties of nuts and seeds can be used to make milk, but in my humble opinion, whole raw cashews produce the mildest, creamiest milk with just the right amount of natural sweetness that additional sweeteners are generally unnecessary. However, if you've adapted to commercial nut milks with sweeteners for drinking purposes, this milk may taste a bit bland and a natural sweetener can always be added to suit your taste. This recipe yields about 1 quart of raw cashew milk. Raw cashew milk has a refrigerator shelf life of up to 5 days.

Ingredients:

- 1 cup (5 oz by weight) whole raw cashews
- 3 and ½ cups filtered or spring water
- ¼ tsp fine sea salt or kosher salt

You will also need a blender and a nylon nut milk bag to strain the fine solids from the milk. A strainer lined with 4-layers of cheesecloth and a large spoon can be used in place of the nut milk bag.

Technique:

Rinse the cashews to remove any dust or debris, drain thoroughly and place them in a high-powered blender. Pre-soaking of the cashews is not required. Add the salt and process the contents on high speed for 2 full minutes.

The milk will now need to be strained to remove the solids. To do this, wash your hands thoroughly and then pour the milk into the nut milk bag over a large container.

While holding the top of the bag with one hand, gently knead the bag to help the milk pass through the ultra-fine mesh - but don't force the milk through.

Optionally, the milk can be poured (in increments) into a strainer lined with 4-layers of cheesecloth placed over a large container. Stir the milk gently with a spoon to help it pass through the layers of cheesecloth.

Cashews break down significantly when processed into milk, so there won't be much solid residue remaining in the nut milk bag or strainer (compared to soymilk or almond milk, which leaves a great deal of solid residue). Discard or compost the cashew solids.

Sweeten the milk to taste, if desired. Transfer to a sealable container and refrigerate. Shake well before using.

Chocolate Cashew Milk and Hot Chocolate

Kids will love this recipe and your "inner child" will love it too. Chocolate cashew milk is delicious served cold and is ideal for preparing hot chocolate because it naturally thickens when heated. This recipe yields about 1 quart of chocolate cashew milk. Chocolate cashew milk has a refrigerator shelf life of up to 5 days.

Ingredients:

- 1 cup (5 oz by weight) whole raw cashews
- 3 and ½ cups filtered or spring water
- ⅔ cup organic sugar, or more to taste
- ⅓ cup unsweetened cocoa powder
- 1 tsp real vanilla extract
- ¼ tsp fine sea salt or kosher salt

You will also need a blender and a nylon nut milk bag to strain the fine solids from the milk. A strainer lined with 4-layers of cheesecloth and a large spoon can be used in place of the nut milk bag.

Technique:

Rinse the cashews to remove any dust or debris, drain thoroughly and place them in a high-powered blender. Pre-soaking of the cashews is not required. Process the contents on high speed for 2 full minutes.

The milk will now need to be strained to remove the solids. To do this, wash your hands thoroughly and then pour the milk into the nut milk bag over a large container. While holding the top of the bag with one hand, gently knead the bag to help the milk pass through the ultra-fine mesh, but don't force the milk through.

Optionally, the milk can be poured (in increments) into a strainer lined with 4-layers of cheesecloth placed over a large container. Stir the milk gently with a spoon to help it pass through the cheesecloth. Pour the strained milk back into the blender and discard or compost the solids in the bag or cheesecloth.

Add the sugar to taste, cocoa powder, vanilla and salt to the blender and process until smooth. Store the milk in a covered container in the refrigerator. Shake well before serving.

For hot chocolate, gently heat the chocolate cashew milk in a saucepan while continually stirring. Do not let the milk boil!

Top the hot chocolate with Marshmallows (pg. 147), Whipped Crème (pg. 25) or Whipped Coconut Cream (pg. 27), if desired.

Almond Milk

Commercial almond milk can be purchased easily enough, but commercial versions usually include a significant amount of sweeteners, emulsifiers and stabilizers to keep them homogenized, and thickeners to compensate for their watery consistency.

Almond meal/flour, blanched almonds or whole raw almonds can be used to prepare almond milk at home. Homemade almond milk has a mild, nutty flavor and slightly astringent aroma. It has a rich consistency that is very different from its commercial counterpart and is the only recommended alternative to soymilk for preparing Better Butter and the Block and Wheel Cheeses in this cookbook.

Unblanched whole raw almonds can be used if preferred, but be aware that the almond skins can impart a bitter undertaste. Almond milk lacks the natural sweetness of raw cashew milk; therefore, for drinking purposes a natural sweetener can be added to suit your taste.

Almond meal/flour requires no presoaking prior to preparation; however blanched almonds or whole raw almonds require presoaking in water for a minimum of 8 hours to soften them before processing. This recipe yields 1 quart of fresh almond milk. Almond milk has a refrigerator shelf life of up to 5 days.

Ingredients:

- 3 and ¾ cup water
- 1 packed cup almond meal/flour; or 5 oz. blanched almonds
- ¼ tsp fine sea salt or kosher salt

You will also need a blender and a nylon nut milk bag to strain the fine solids from the milk. A strainer lined with 4-layers of cheesecloth and a large spoon can be used in place of the nut milk bag.

Technique:

If using blanched almonds, or whole raw almonds, place them into a container with a lid and add plenty of water to cover. Refrigerate for a minimum of 8 hours to soften. Drain and discard the soaking water and add the almonds to a blender with 3 and ¾ cup fresh water and the salt. If using almond meal/flour, presoaking is unnecessary. Add the almond meal/flour directly to the blender with the water and the salt. Process the contents on high speed for 2 full minutes.

The milk will now need to be strained to remove the solids. To do this, wash your hands thoroughly and then pour the milk into the nut milk bag over a large container.

While holding the top of the bag with one hand, vigorously knead the bag to help the milk pass through the ultra-fine mesh, squeezing as much of the milk as possible from the ground almonds.

Optionally, the milk can be poured (in increments) into a strainer lined with 4-layers of cheesecloth placed over a large container. Stir and press with a spoon to help the milk pass through the layers of cheesecloth.

Almonds don't break down as easily as cashews when preparing milk, so there will be a significant amount of residue remaining in the nut milk bag or strainer. Discard or compost the solids or reserve for other uses (for example, it can be dried and used for Grated Parmesan, pg. 99).

For drinking purposes, sweeten the milk to taste; it will need it. Transfer the milk to a sealable container and refrigerate. Like other nut milks, almond milk has a tendency to separate upon standing. Shake well before using.

Rice Milk

Rice milk is made from brown rice and is especially useful for those with sensitivities to soymilk or nut milks. It's higher in carbohydrates than soy or nut milks and has a rather distinct (but not unpleasant) starchy flavor. When lightly sweetened, it is very palatable for drinking and is especially good for pouring over cold cereal. Rice milk is ideal for making Horchata (recipe follows), a sweetened Latin American beverage flavored with cinnamon and vanilla. This recipe yields about 1 quart. Rice milk has a refrigerator shelf life of up to 7 days.

Ingredients:

- ⅓ cup organic long grain brown rice
- 4 and ½ cups water
- 1 T organic sugar or other natural sweetener, or more to taste
- 1 T mild vegetable oil
- ¼ tsp fine sea salt or kosher salt

You will also need a blender, cooking tongs and a nylon nut milk bag to strain the fine solids from the milk. A strainer lined with 4-layers of cheesecloth and a large spoon can be used in place of the nut milk bag and cooking tongs.

Technique:

Rinse the rice thoroughly in a strainer and add to a large saucepan. Add the water, sugar, oil and optional salt and bring to a rapid boil. Stir, cover and reduce the heat to low. Cook for 45 minutes. Let the rice mixture cool for about 30 minutes before proceeding.

Pour the rice mixture into a blender, put the lid in place and cover the lid with a dish towel (to prevent steam burns). Begin blending on low speed, slowly increasing to high speed and process for 2 full minutes. Let the mixture cool for an additional 30 minutes.

The milk will now need to be strained to remove the solids. Pour the milk into the nut milk bag over a large container. The milk will still be hot, so cooking tongs will come in handy for the next step. While holding the top of the bag with one hand, gently squeeze the bag repeatedly with the tongs to help the milk pass through the ultra-fine mesh.

Optionally, the milk can be poured into a strainer lined with 4-layers of cheesecloth placed over a large container. Stir the milk with a large spoon to help it pass through the cheesecloth. Discard or compost the solids in the bag or cheesecloth. Transfer the milk to a sealable container and refrigerate. Shake well before using.

Horchata

Horchata is a sweetened Latin American rice beverage flavored with cinnamon and vanilla. It is served chilled over crushed ice. For this recipe, you will need 1 quart of strained, warm rice milk prepared from the previous recipe.

To prepare Horchata, mix together 1 tsp ground cinnamon and 2 tsp real vanilla extract in the bottom of a 1 quart container. Add 1 quart of strained, warm rice milk. Stir in an additional 2 tablespoons organic sugar and ¼ cup real maple syrup and mix thoroughly to dissolve the sugar. Chill and serve over crushed ice.

Non-Dairy Creams

Crēme

For many years, cashew cream was my "go to" cream for cooking and adding to hot beverages. However, in my experience the powerful thickening properties of cashew cream when heated was undesirable for preparing delicate cream-based sauces. And no matter how thoroughly the cashew cream was strained, there was always a subtle but discernible grittiness on the tongue when added to hot beverages such as tea and coffee.

Convenience was also a factor, since whole raw cashews are not generally available in supermarkets. They're also rather expensive unless purchased in bulk. Preparing cashew cream takes time too, since the cashews require soaking prior to preparation and then straining the mixture after processing. It seemed I never had cashew cream on hand when I wanted to prepare a recipe without pre-planning.

So I began researching the properties of dairy cream to find a solution. Dairy cream is a product that is composed of the higher-butterfat layer skimmed from the top of whole milk before homogenization.

Soymilk serves as the base for this cream since it is a stable emulsion containing approximately the same proportion of protein, fat and carbohydrates as low-fat cow's milk; and because organic refined coconut oil shares similar properties with dairy butterfat, it serves as the ideal fat. The soymilk and coconut oil are emulsified together using a blender and the stability of the soymilk enables the cream to remain homogenized. By adjusting the milk-to-fat ratio, the cream can be prepared in various fat densities, ranging from heavy whipping cream to light cream.

I've tested Crēme extensively in many cooking applications, and have found that it behaves exactly like dairy cream in both hot and cold foods. It has a silky smooth texture and is very quick and easy to prepare. Crēme has a refrigerator shelf life of up to 10 days, as opposed to cashew cream which has a shelf life of up to 5 days. With such ease of preparation and a longer shelf life, one can always have it on hand when needed. Each formula yields 2 cups of the finest non-dairy cream. To produce 1 quart, simply double the formula measurements.

Important! Omit the sweetener and salt in the formula if using home prepared soymilk that already has sweetener and salt added.

Basic Crēme (ideal for most cooking purposes):

- 1 and ½ cup pure soymilk, room temperature
- ½ cup organic **refined** coconut oil
- 1 tsp organic sugar or other natural sweetener
- ⅛ tsp fine sea salt or kosher salt

Light Crēme (ideal for preparing ice cream and as a creamer for hot or cold beverages; for sweetened and flavored coffee creamers, please see the recipes on page 21 and 23):

- 1 and ¾ cup pure soymilk, room temperature
- ¼ cup organic **refined** coconut oil
- 1 tsp organic sugar or other natural sweetener
- ⅛ tsp fine sea salt or kosher salt

Heavy Crēme (ideal for any recipe calling for heavy dairy cream)

- 1 and ⅓ cup pure soymilk, room temperature
- ⅔ cup organic **refined** coconut oil

- 1 tsp organic sugar or other natural sweetener
- ⅛ tsp fine sea salt or kosher salt

For **Heavy Whipping Crēme**, please see the formula and instructions on page 25.

Technique:

The soymilk must be at room temperature to emulsify properly with the coconut oil. If necessary, gently warm the milk in a saucepan over low heat or briefly in the microwave. If cold soymilk is used, the coconut oil will congeal when it comes into contact with the cold liquid and disrupt the emulsification process.

Remove the metal lid from the jar of coconut oil and place the jar in a microwave. Heat just until the solid oil liquefies, about 30 seconds to 1 minute (this will depend upon the solidity of the coconut oil). Alternately, place the jar in about an inch of simmering water and melt the oil in the same manner. Measure the coconut oil and set aside.

Pour the milk into a blender and cover. Begin blending on low speed, gradually increasing to high speed (if the milk is splashing too much in the blender jar, reduce the speed slightly). Pour the coconut oil **slowly** into the milk through the opening in the blender jar's lid. Continue to run the blender for about 10 seconds on high speed after the oil has been added to ensure that the cream is completely homogenized.

Transfer the cream to a sealable container and refrigerate until well-chilled. The cream will thicken to the proper texture upon refrigeration. Shake well before using and consume within 10 days.

Quick Crème Fraîche

Quick Crème Fraîche is an uncultured, soy-based soured cream which is quickly and easily prepared using Basic Crēme and lactic acid powder. It naturally thickens on its own without added food starches, gums or gels.

It has a lighter viscosity than American-style sour cream but will work for most recipes just as you would sour cream. This recipe yields 1 cup.

Ingredients:

- 1 cup Basic Crēme, chilled (see preceding recipe)
- ¾ tsp lactic acid powder (sorry, no substitutions for this recipe)
- ¼ tsp fine sea salt or kosher salt

Technique:

Whisk together the ingredients in a bowl. Thickening will begin instantaneously. Cover and refrigerate for a minimum of 1 hour to ensure full thickening. Various chopped fresh herbs can be stirred in prior to serving if desired, to accommodate various ethnic cuisines (cilantro Crème Fraîche, for example, is an excellent topping for Tex-Mex Cuisine).

Sweetened Coffee Creamer #1
(Soy-Based with Optional Flavors)

This recipe yields 2 cups of the finest, sweetened non-dairy coffee creamer. The creamer can also be flavored with several delicious options. For unsweetened creamer, omit the sweetener and optional flavorings. Sweetened coffee creamer has a shelf life of up to 10 days.

Ingredients:

- ¼ cup organic **refined** coconut oil
- 1 and ¾ cup pure soymilk (sorry, no substitutions)
- ¼ cup organic sugar or natural sweetener of your choice

Flavor variations:

- ❖ For mocha creamer, add 2 T unsweetened cocoa powder (or carob powder) before blending.
- ❖ For French vanilla creamer, add 4 tsp real vanilla extract before blending.
- ❖ For cinnamon streusel creamer, add 1 tsp ground cinnamon and 1 T real vanilla extract before blending.
- ❖ For pumpkin spice creamer, add 1 tsp pumpkin pie spice and 1 tsp real vanilla extract before blending.

Technique:

Remove the metal lid from the jar of coconut oil and place the jar in a microwave. Heat just until the solid oil liquefies, about 30 seconds to 1 minute (this will depend upon the solidity of the coconut oil). Alternately, place the jar in about an inch of simmering water and melt the oil in the same manner. Measure the coconut oil and set aside.

Pour the milk into a blender and add the optional sugar and/or flavoring ingredients. Cover and begin blending on low speed, gradually increasing to high speed (if the milk is splashing too much in the blender jar, reduce the speed slightly). Pour the coconut oil **slowly** into the milk through the opening in the blender jar's lid. Continue to run the blender for about 10 seconds on high speed after the oil has been added to ensure that the cream is completely homogenized.

Transfer to a sealable container and refrigerate for several hours until chilled. Shake well before using.

Cashew Cream

Cashew cream is essentially concentrated cashew milk. It is prepared by processing whole raw cashews with a reduced amount of water and then straining to remove the heavier nut solids. Although I recommend soy-based Crēme for most cooking applications, cashew cream can be used in recipes if soy is not an option. Cashew cream has powerful thickening properties when heated and can quickly over-thicken delicate sauces. To use cashew cream for this purpose, whisk the cashew cream into the sauce just before serving and avoid additional heating. Cashew cream has a shelf life of 4 to 5 days. This recipe yields about 2 cups.

Ingredients:

- 1 cup (5 oz by weight) whole raw cashews
- 1 and ½ cup water
- ⅛ tsp fine sea salt or kosher salt

Technique:

Place the cashews into a container with a lid and add plenty of water to cover. Refrigerate for a minimum of 8 hours to soften. Drain and discard the soaking water and add the cashews to a blender with 1 and ½ cup fresh water and the salt; process on high speed for 2 full minutes.

The cream will now need to be strained to remove the larger suspended solids. To do this, wash your hands thoroughly and pour the cream into the nut milk bag over a large bowl or pitcher.

While holding the top of the bag with one hand, gently knead the bag to help the cream pass through the ultra-fine mesh but avoid forcing the cream through. Discard or compost any solids in the bag.

Optionally, the cream can be poured (in increments) into a strainer lined with 4 layers of cheesecloth. Stir the cream gently with a spoon to help it pass through the cheesecloth. Transfer the cream to a sealable container and refrigerate. Shake well before using.

Sweetened Coffee Creamer #2
(Cashew-Based)

While my soy-based coffee creamer provides the smoothest texture for hot and cold beverages, cashew creamer is an option for individuals who are allergic to soy. This recipe yields about 2 cups of naturally sweetened coffee creamer.

Ingredients:

- 2 cups plain or vanilla non-dairy milk
- ½ cup (2.5 oz. by weight) whole raw cashews
- 6 pitted dates

You will also need a high-powered blender and a nut milk bag or a fine mesh strainer lined with 4 layers of cheesecloth to strain the solids from the cream.

*For mocha creamer, use chocolate non-dairy milk. For unsweetened creamer, use plain non-dairy milk and omit the dates.

Technique:

Rinse the cashews to remove any dust or debris and drain thoroughly. Place the milk, cashews and dates into a container with a lid, seal and place in the refrigerator to soak for a minimum of 8 hours. After soaking, transfer the ingredients to a blender and process on high speed for 2 full minutes.

The cream will now need to be strained to remove the suspended particles. To do this, wash your hands thoroughly and then pour the cream into the nut milk bag over a large bowl or pitcher.

While holding the top of the bag with one hand, gently knead the bag to help the cream pass through the ultra-fine mesh; avoid forcing the cream through. Discard or compost the solids in the bag.

Cashew cream has a subtle but discernible gritty texture when used in hot and cold beverages, so to ensure the smoothest cream, strain the cream again.

Optionally, the cream can be poured (in increments) into a strainer lined with 4 layers of cheesecloth. Stir the cream with a spoon to help it pass through the cheesecloth.

Transfer the cream to a sealable container and refrigerate. Shake well before using.

Chai Thai Iced Tea

This refreshing beverage is a unique variation of the popular sweetened iced tea served in Thai restaurants.

Chai is a South Asian flavored tea beverage made by brewing black tea with a mixture of aromatic Indian herbs and spices.

The black tea infusion itself is less concentrated than the tea used for making traditional Thai iced tea. The layers of sweetened cream and fragrant and sweet Chai tea make a lovely presentation. This recipe serves 2.

Ingredients:

- 6 teabags of Ceylon black tea (or any strong black tea) (decaffeinated if you prefer, or a combination of both)
- 1 and ½ cup boiling water
- 1 thin slice of fresh ginger root
- 1 piece star anise (or ½ tsp fennel or anise seed)
- 2 whole cloves
- 2 pods green cardamom
- 2 black peppercorns
- ½ stick cinnamon
- 1 T organic sugar, or more to taste
- crushed ice
- Sweetened Coffee Creamer (see preceding recipes)
- mint leaves for garnish (optional)

Simple version:

- 6 teabags of spiced Chai tea (such as Bigelow's Spiced Chai Tea ™) (decaffeinated if you prefer, or a combination of both)
- 1 and ½ cup boiling water
- 1 T organic sugar, or more to taste
- crushed ice
- Sweetened Coffee Creamer (see preceding recipes)
- mint leaves for garnish (optional)

Technique:

Steep the teabags and spices in the boiling hot water until cooled. Add the sugar while the tea is still warm and stir to dissolve.

Add 2 to 3 tablespoons of creamer to the bottom of each glass. Fill the glasses with crushed ice and then strain ¾ cup of tea into each glass. Serve with the optional mint garnish.

Heavy Whipping Crème

At last, a non-dairy whipping cream that whips just like dairy whipping cream! The whipped cream produced from this recipe has a lighter texture and mouth feel comparable to dairy whipped cream, as opposed to the dense texture of whipped coconut cream. Regardless, consume moderately as this is not a low fat or low calorie topping! This recipe yields 2 cups of heavy whipping cream which will produce about 3 cups of the finest non-dairy whipped cream.

Ingredients for the Heavy Whipping Crème:

- 1 cup pure soymilk, room temperature
- 1 cup organic refined or virgin coconut oil*

For whipping the Heavy Whipping Crème, you will need:

- ⅓ cup Organic Powdered Sugar (see following recipe) or similar
- 1 tsp real vanilla extract

Special equipment needed:

- ceramic or metal mixing bowl
- stand mixer with balloon whip attachment or electric rotary hand mixer

*Please note that virgin coconut oil will impart a subtle coconut undertaste.

Technique:

The soymilk must be at room temperature to emulsify properly with the coconut oil. If necessary, gently warm the milk in a saucepan over low heat or briefly in the microwave. If cold soymilk is used, the coconut oil will congeal when it comes into contact with the cold liquid.

Remove the metal lid from the jar of coconut oil and place the jar in a microwave. Heat just until the solid oil liquefies, about 30 seconds to 1 minute (this will depend upon the solidity of the coconut oil). Alternately, place the jar in about an inch of simmering water and melt the oil in the same manner. Measure the coconut oil and set aside.

Pour the milk into a blender and cover. Begin blending on low speed, gradually increasing to high speed (if the milk is splashing too much in the blender jar, reduce the speed slightly). Pour the coconut oil **slowly** into the milk through the opening in the blender jar's lid. Continue to run the blender for about 10 seconds on high speed after the oil has been added to ensure that the cream is completely homogenized.

Pour the Heavy Whipping Crème into a sealable container and refrigerate until **very cold** before whipping.

Preparing Whipped Crème

Place a metal or ceramic mixing bowl and 2 beaters from an electric rotary mixer or the metal bowl and balloon whip attachment from a stand mixer into the refrigerator. Chill until **very cold**. Blenders and food processors will not work for this recipe, as they will not whip air into the Heavy Whipping Crème.

Pour the Heavy Whipping Crème into the chilled bowl and begin whipping with the electric mixer or stand mixer on low speed, gradually increasing to high speed. Whip until soft peaks begin to form. This will take 3 to 5 minutes, so be patient. Begin incorporating the powdered sugar, in increments, and add the vanilla. Continue to whip until stiff peaks form.

Transfer the Whipped Crēme to a covered container and refrigerate until ready to use. Whipped Crēme will retain its whipped texture as long as it is refrigerated. Consume within 7 to 10 days.

Organic Powdered Sugar

Why make your own powdered sugar? Unless you specifically purchase organic powdered sugar, the majority of commercial powdered sugar available is produced from refined white sugar which has typically been filtered through animal bone char during the refining process. Making your own is very simple. The powdered sugar has starch added, at 3%, which is commonly used as an anti-caking agent. This recipe yields about 1 lb. of powdered sugar.

Ingredients:

- 2 cups organic sugar (evaporated cane juice)
- 1 T cornstarch or unmodified potato starch

Technique:

In a DRY blender, add the sugar and starch and process at high speed into a very fine powder. Store the sugar in an airtight, dry container until ready to use.

Whipped Coconut Cream

This rich and creamy whipped topping is superb for topping non-dairy desserts.

Coconut cream is the solid fat that rises to the top of full-fat coconut milk when chilled. "Creamed coconut" and "cream of coconut" are not the same as pure coconut cream, since they often contain sugar and additional ingredients including fragments of coconut meat. Coconut manna is also a different "whole food" coconut product; in other words, it contains the coconut meat as well as the cream.

The amount of coconut cream in coconut milk will vary from brand to brand and even from can to can. Look for the words "first-pressing" on the can, as this is usually a good indicator (but not always) that the can will contain more coconut cream. Two 13.5 oz cans of organic, unsweetened, full-fat coconut milk should yield enough cream for this recipe. However, depending upon the yield of the brand you are using, you may need additional cans. I have had the most consistent amount of coconut cream per can using Native Forest™ organic coconut milk. Canned pure coconut cream is also available for convenience. Native Forest™ offers pure organic coconut cream in 5.4 oz. cans. Trader Joe's also offers pure coconut cream.

Enjoy but consume moderately as this is not a low fat or low calorie topping! Please note that coconut cream does impart a subtle coconut undertaste; if this is an issue, opt for the soy-based whipped cream prepared from the recipe on page 25. This recipe yields about 2 cups of whipped coconut cream.

Ingredients:

- 1 and ½ cup solid coconut cream
- ⅓ cup Organic Powdered Sugar (see preceding recipe)
- 1 tsp real vanilla extract

Special equipment needed:

- ceramic or metal mixing bowl
- stand mixer with balloon whip attachment or electric rotary hand mixer

Technique:

Chill the cans of coconut milk towards the back of the refrigerator for a minimum of 48 hours. The cans must get as cold as possible without freezing. This will ensure that the cream is completely solidified and separated from the coconut water.

Place a metal or ceramic mixing bowl and 2 beaters from an electric rotary mixer or the metal bowl and balloon whip attachment from a stand mixer into the refrigerator. Chill until **very cold**. Blenders and food processors will not work for this recipe, as they will not whip air into the cream.

Open the top of the cans with a can opener, leaving a small hinge for the lids to stay attached. Scoop out the solidified cream until you reach the coconut water and place in the mixing bowl. If using a good quality coconut milk, there should be a substantial amount of cream. Close the lid and drain the coconut water, reserving for another use if desired (smoothies perhaps?) **Do not add the coconut water to the mixing bowl!**

Open the can and scoop out any remaining cream that may have solidified near the bottom of the can (if any) and add to the mixing bowl. Add the vanilla and powdered sugar to the cream and fold in to combine.

Beat the mixture on high-speed for several minutes until the mixture is thick, smooth and peaks begin to form. Transfer to an air-tight container and refrigerate until ready to use. The whipped cream will stay firm as long as it is refrigerated.

Non-Dairy Butter

Better Butter

Better Butter is a superior tasting, palm oil-free alternative to dairy butter and commercial non-dairy margarine. This recipe produces a buttery spread that looks, tastes and melts like dairy butter and can be used in any recipe, including baking, as you would dairy butter. Just like its dairy counterpart, Better Butter browns and burns when exposed to high heat and therefore should not be used for high-heat sautéing - it works best with low to medium heat.

The best kitchen appliance for emulsifying the butter ingredients is an immersion blender or food processor. The ingredients can also be emulsified using a standard or high-speed blender; however, retrieving the thick butter from around the blades can be difficult. This recipe yields about 2 cups of butter.

Ingredients:

- 1 cup organic **refined** coconut oil
- ⅓ cup mild vegetable oil
- ⅔ cup pure soymilk or homemade Almond Milk (pg. 17)
- 4 tsp/20 ml liquid soy lecithin or liquid sunflower lecithin*;
  or 24 grams/.8 oz. soy or sunflower lecithin powder (about 2 T plus 2 tsp);
  or 24 grams/.8 oz. soy or sunflower lecithin granules ground into a fine powder
- 1 tsp organic sugar
- ½ tsp lactic acid powder**
- ¼ tsp to 1 tsp fine sea salt or kosher salt, to taste
- ½ tsp nutritional yeast flakes
- ½ tsp guar gum, sodium alginate or xanthan gum

*Sunflower lecithin can be substituted for the soy lecithin for those who prefer a soy-free butter. However, sunflower lecithin lacks the rich golden hue of soy lecithin, so expect a color variation.

**Lactic acid powder can be substituted with 1 tsp raw apple cider vinegar and 1 tsp fresh lemon juice.

Technique:

You will need a 2-cup minimum food storage container with a lid to store the butter. If you prefer, the butter can be shaped in a flexible silicone form, or divided into several forms, and released after hardening.

First, remove the metal lid from the jar of coconut oil and place the jar in a microwave. Heat just until the solid oil liquefies, about 30 seconds to 1 minute (this will depend upon the solidity of the coconut oil). Alternately, place the jar in about an inch of simmering water and melt the oil in the same manner.

Pour 1 cup of the coconut oil into a 2-cup measuring cup or other suitable container with a pouring "lip". Add ⅓ cup vegetable oil to the coconut oil and set aside.

Immersion blender method:

Add the remaining ingredients to a 4-cup glass measuring cup or heavy glass/ceramic bowl. Insert the immersion blender and process the mixture for about 15 seconds.

Now, with the immersion blender running on high speed, begin slowly pouring the mixed oils into the blending cup or bowl. Move the blender up and down and side to side as you add the oils. Continue blending until the mixture is emulsified and thick. Transfer to a sealable container, cover and freeze until solid (if using one or several silicone molds, cover with plastic wrap).

Once frozen, place the butter in the refrigerator until thawed before using; or it can be stored in the freezer for up to 3 months. To release the butter from a form, simply wiggle the sides a bit to loosen and then press out onto a plate.

Food processor method:

Add the remaining ingredients to the processor and turn on the processor. Now begin to slowly pour the mixed oils into the mixture through the food chute. Continue to process until the mixture is emulsified and thick. Transfer to a sealable container, cover and freeze until solid (if using one or several silicone molds, cover with plastic wrap).

Once frozen, place the butter in the refrigerator until thawed before using; or it can be stored in the freezer for up to 3 months. To release the butter from a form, simply wiggle the sides a bit to loosen and then press out onto a plate.

Seasoned Butter

Seasoned Butter is a blend of homemade butter and specially selected herbs and spices. It's wonderful for adding a flavorful crust to pan-seared seitan cutlets, tofu or tempeh. It's also excellent for topping potatoes, corn on the cob, cooked grains and cooked vegetables.

Ingredients:

- ½ cup Better Butter (pg. 28) or Vital Butter (pg. 33), room temperature
- 1 T fresh lemon juice
- 1 tsp vegan Worcestershire sauce
- ½ tsp onion powder
- ½ tsp garlic powder
- ¼ tsp coarse ground black pepper
- ¼ tsp sweet paprika
- ¼ tsp fine sea salt or kosher salt
- 2 tsp minced fresh herbs of your choice (optional)

Technique:

Mash all ingredients together in a bowl. Refrigerate in a covered container until ready to use.

Cultured Butter, Buttermilk and Creams

Rejuvelac

Rejuvelac is a non-alcoholic fermented liquid made from sprouted grains. It is an inexpensive and easy-to-make probiotic rich in lactobacilli, nutrients and enzymes. Drinking a small amount each day is very beneficial to the digestive system, promoting a healthy intestinal flora. However, in this book it is specifically used to culture cashew milk and cashew cream for producing the finest non-dairy butter, buttermilk, sour cream, and cashew-based cheeses.

Some people prepare rejuvelac using different types of grain, but I prefer organic white wheat berries (raw wheat) and the process works perfectly every time. You may come across different varieties of wheat when shopping for wheat berries, such as hard or soft, red or white, or spring or winter. I have had success with all forms; as long as it sprouts, it will work. If you have gluten intolerance, wheat berries can still be used for preparing rejuvelac, since the gluten protein in wheat isn't activated until the wheat is ground into flour and cooked. However, if this makes you nervous, raw quinoa works well.

If you choose to work with quinoa or other grains, do some internet research on preparing rejuvelac with that particular grain, since the amount of grain used and soaking and preparation times may be different than wheat. Please be aware that brown rice needs special conditions like high sustained temperatures to sprout; and some grains, such as oats and buckwheat, are often processed to render them "unsproutable".

So exactly how does this process work? Prior to its decay, plant material begins to ferment (a bacterial ferment, not an alcoholic ferment). When the sprouted grain sits in standing water, an anaerobic environment (lack of oxygen) occurs and the lactobacillus bacteria, which are present everywhere in the environment around us, begin to grow.

Lactobacillus is a genus of anaerobic rod-shaped bacteria. "Lacto" refers to their ability to convert lactose (milk sugar) and other sugars to lactic acid. Eventually the bacteria produce so much acid that decay bacteria cannot survive. Lactic acid is the compound responsible for souring milk and producing sharp flavors in cheese. Various strains of lactobacillus are also used for the production of yogurt, sauerkraut, pickles, beer, wine, hard cider, kimchi, cocoa, and other fermented foods.

I'm often asked if vegan acidophilus powder or other probiotic capsules can substitute for rejuvelac in making cultured non-dairy products. My answer is "no" because rejuvelac is fresh and biologically potent. It also contains several wild strains of lactobacillus, as well as living enzymes and other nutrients which impart complex lactic flavors to cultured non-dairy foods. However, specific strains of freeze-dried lacto-cultures are advantageous for use as a yogurt starter.

I've also been asked if kombucha will work as a substitute for rejuvelac. The answer is also "no", at least not for the cultured foods in this cookbook. Although kombucha contains symbiotic colonies of bacteria and yeast, they are entirely different than the lacto-bacterial cultures present in rejuvelac. Kombucha cultures produce acetic acid (vinegar), which accounts for it flavor. In the same manner, rejuvelac does not work for culturing yogurt, because certain strains of bacteria are required. Just because something contains a live culture, does not mean it will work in all culturing applications.

Rejuvelac has a mild, yeast-like aroma and a slightly tart, lemony flavor. Organic white wheat berries can usually be found in health or natural food stores, or purchased online through food retail websites such as Amazon.com. Preparation can take anywhere from 3 to 6 days from start to finish (depending upon ambient room temperature), so plan accordingly and always keep plenty of rejuvelac on hand. This formula will yield approximately 3 and ½ cups of rejuvelac. To double the amount, 1 cup of wheat berries can be soaked and sprouted in a single jar, and the grains divided and fermented in 2 separate jars.

I have gone into great detail to explain the process for preparing rejuvelac; but don't let this lengthy explanation discourage preparation. It really is very simple to prepare once you understand the process.

Ingredients and supplies:

- ½ cup dry organic wheat berries (raw wheat)
- filtered or spring water - DO NOT use tap water!
- 1 quart mason jar (home canning jar)
- 1 six-inch square of double layered cheesecloth and 1 lid ring
  or 1 stainless steel or plastic sprouting lid (available in health foods stores or through the internet)

Technique:

First, before you begin, it is important that anything that comes into contact with the grain (your hands, utensils and containers) be washed thoroughly to prevent contamination of the culture. Cleanliness ensures efficient culturing of the grain (in other words, the lactobacillus bacteria will not have to compete with undesirable organisms).

To prepare the rejuvelac, place ½ cup whole wheat berries in a clean mason jar and fill with filtered or spring water (use 1 cup wheat berries to double the amount of rejuvelac). Do not use tap water as it may contain traces of chlorine which will prevent fermentation. Swirl the contents, let the grains settle to the bottom and carefully pour off the water from the jar.

Now fill the jar with filtered or spring water again, place a square of double-layer cheesecloth over the mouth of the jar and screw the lid ring in place (or use a sprouting lid). Let the grains soak at room temperature for 8 to 12 hours. DO NOT exceed 12 hours or the germ of the wheat can actually drown and die.

After soaking, thoroughly drain and discard the water by pouring through the cheesecloth or sprouting lid. Turn the jar on its side and gently shake to distribute the grains along the bottom. Place the jar in an area that will receive light during the day, but out of direct sunlight.

Twice a day for 2 to 3 days (until the grain sprouts), add filtered or spring water to the jar through the cheesecloth or sprouting lid, swirl, pour out the water and again shake to distribute the grains on the bottom and set the jar on its side. In the warmer summer months, rinse three to four times a day. You should see little tails emerging from the grains on the second or third day. There is no need to let the grains sprout further; proceed to the next step.

Once the little tails have appeared on a large percentage of the grain, rinse a final time with filtered or spring water. Fill the jar with filtered or spring water, place a fresh square of cheesecloth over the mouth of the jar and secure with the lid ring (or use a sprouting lid). If the amount of grain was doubled, pour approximately half the grain from the one jar into the second jar. Fill both jars with filtered or spring water and cover.

Set the jar(s) in an upright position, ideally in a cool place. Fermentation will take anywhere from 24 to 72 hours at room temperature.

The ideal temperature for fermentation is between 68°F to 70°F (which is the same ideal temperature range for preparing sauerkraut). At temperatures over 70°F, fermentation begins to accelerate and there is a risk of pathogenic bacteria overrunning the culture before the lactobacillus bacteria has had a chance to populate. At temperatures under 60°F, fermentation may not occur at all.

I have had the best results with fermentation during the cooler autumn, winter and early spring months. During cooler weather, the rejuvelac can ferment for the full 72 hours without becoming rancid. Longer fermentation at cooler temperatures produces a more potent rejuvelac with less chance of rancidity. In the later spring and summer months however, even when the house feels comfortable, the rejuvelac ferments much quicker, usually within 24 to 36 hours and there is still a risk of rancidity. Therefore, to reduce the risk of spoilage, place the jar(s) in the coolest area of your home during fermentation.

The liquid will turn slightly cloudy as the grain ferments. If you agitate the jar(s) gently, you will begin to notice gas bubbles rising from the grain. This is carbon dioxide being released as a by-product of fermentation. A small amount of foam may also collect near the surface during fermentation; this is normal.

Check the jar(s) every 24 hours and smell the mixture through the cheesecloth or lid. It should have a mild, earthy and grassy aroma; if at any point it begins to smell putrid, discard. You will definitely know if it has turned rancid, as it will have a distinct vomit-like odor.

How will you know when the culture is ready? After 24 to 72 hours of fermentation time (depending upon ambient temperature), the resulting culture should be releasing a substantial amount of bubbles when the jar is gently agitated. This is the best way to gauge its biological activity. Use a clean spoon and taste the liquid. The flavor should have just the slightest hint of lemon. If you have a sensitive palate, it may also feel slightly fizzy on your tongue, like a weak carbonated beverage.

When ready, pour the liquid from the grain jar(s) through the cheesecloth or sprouting lid into a clean container or pitcher with a lid, loosely secure the container lid in place and refrigerate. It is important to leave the container lid slightly loose since the mixture will continue to release small amounts of carbon dioxide gas and the resulting pressure needs to escape.

Discard the grain (preferably via composting or feeding to small animals). Rejuvelac can be stored in the refrigerator for about 2 weeks; however, fresh rejuvelac is more potent and it will begin to lose potency the longer it is refrigerated.

During refrigeration, sediment may form at the bottom of the container; this is normal. Simply decant the liquid for use in recipes and discard the sediment at the bottom. The liquid may also begin to darken slightly after a period of time in the refrigerator. This is also normal. However, if the rejuvelac begins to smell like vinegar, or develops a very strong sour taste, it has expired and needs to be discarded. Always test the flavor of rejuvelac for freshness before using in a recipe.

Some of my readers have reported success with freezing rejuvelac while still maintaining viability of the culture. While I recommend using fresh rejuvelac, freezing may be a storage option if you wish to experiment.

Vital Butter

Vital Butter is a cultured, cashew-based, palm oil-free butter with a flavor that is remarkably similar to artisan-crafted European dairy butter. The lactic acid in this butter is naturally produced during the culturing process of the cashew milk. This natural lactic acid eliminates the need for commercially produced lactic acid (or fruit acids) to add flavor to the butter. My signature recipe produces a butter that looks, tastes and melts like dairy butter and can be used in any recipe, including baked goods, as you would dairy butter.

Since Vital Butter contains live bacterial cultures and enzymes, it is a "living food" and will continue to develop flavor as it chills in the refrigerator, much in the same way that yogurt continues to develop flavor.

Just like its dairy counterpart, Vital Butter browns and burns when exposed to high heat and therefore should not be used for high-heat sautéing; it works best with low to medium heat.

The best kitchen appliance for emulsifying the butter ingredients is an immersion blender. A food processor will also work. The ingredients can also be emulsified using a standard or high-speed blender; however, retrieving the thick butter from around the blades can be difficult. This recipe yields about 2 cups of butter.

Ingredients:

- 1 cup organic **refined** coconut oil
- ⅔ cup Cultured Raw Buttermilk (pg. 34)
- ⅓ cup mild vegetable oil
- 4 tsp/20 ml liquid soy lecithin or liquid sunflower lecithin*;
  or 24 grams/.8 oz. soy or sunflower lecithin powder (about 2 T plus 2 tsp);
  or 24 grams/.8 oz. soy or sunflower lecithin granules ground into a fine powder
- 1 tsp organic sugar
- ¼ tsp to 1 tsp fine sea salt or kosher salt, to taste
- ½ tsp guar gum, sodium alginate or xanthan gum

*Sunflower lecithin can be substituted for the soy lecithin for those who prefer a soy-free butter. However, sunflower lecithin lacks the rich golden hue of soy lecithin, so expect a color variation.

Technique:

You will need a 2-cup minimum food storage container with a lid to store the butter. If you prefer, the butter can be shaped in a flexible silicone form, or divided into several forms, and released after hardening.

First, remove the metal lid from the jar of coconut oil and place the jar in a microwave. Heat just until the solid oil liquefies, about 30 seconds to 1 minute (this will depend upon the solidity of the coconut oil). Alternately, place the jar in about an inch of simmering water and melt the oil in the same manner. Measure 1 cup of the coconut oil into a 2-cup measuring cup or other suitable container with a pouring "lip". Add ⅓ cup vegetable oil to the coconut oil and set aside.

Immersion blender method:

Add the remaining ingredients to a 4-cup glass measuring cup or heavy glass/ceramic bowl. Insert the immersion blender and process the mixture for about 15 seconds.

With the immersion blender running on high speed, begin slowly pouring the mixed oils into the blending cup or bowl. Move the blender gently up and down and side to side as you add the oils. Continue blending until the mixture is emulsified and thick. Transfer to a sealable container, cover and freeze until solid (if using one or several silicone molds, cover with plastic wrap).

Once frozen, place the butter in the refrigerator until thawed before using; or it can be stored in the freezer for up to 3 months. Freezing will not harm the culture. To release the butter from a form, simply wiggle the sides a bit to loosen and then press out onto a plate.

Food processor method:

Add the remaining ingredients to the processor and turn on the processor. Now begin to slowly pour the mixed oils into the mixture through the food chute. Continue to process until the mixture is emulsified and thick. Transfer to a sealable container, cover and freeze until solid (if using one or several silicone molds, cover with plastic wrap).

Once frozen, place the butter in the refrigerator until thawed before using; or it can be stored in the freezer for up to 3 months. Freezing will not harm the culture. To release the butter from a form, simply wiggle the sides a bit to loosen and then press out onto a plate.

Cultured Raw Buttermilk

I realize I'm in the minority, but buttermilk was one of the things I missed the most when I adopted a strict plant-based diet. If you've ever missed drinking a cold glass of refreshing buttermilk, then this recipe is for you too. Cultured raw buttermilk is rich in probiotics and living enzymes which are beneficial for nurturing digestive health. Cultured raw buttermilk is also excellent for raw cuisine and cold food applications, such as Chilled Cucumber Buttermilk Soup (pg. 36), and salad dressings or dips, such as Buttermilk Ranch Dressing and Dip (pg. 35). The cashews do not require pre-soaking. This recipe yields about 1 quart of the finest cultured buttermilk.

Ingredients:

- 1 cup (5 oz by weight) whole raw cashews
- 2 and ½ cups filtered or spring water
- 1 cup Rejuvelac (pg. 30)
- ½ tsp fine sea salt or kosher salt

You will also need a blender and a nylon nut milk bag to strain the fine solids from the buttermilk. A strainer lined with 4-layers of cheesecloth and a large spoon can be used in place of the nut milk bag.

Technique:

Rinse the cashews to remove any dust or debris, drain thoroughly and place them in a high-powered blender. Add 2 and ½ cups of fresh filtered or spring water and the salt and process on high speed for 2 full minutes. Wash your hands thoroughly and then pour the milk into the nut milk bag over a large container.

While holding the top of the bag with one hand, gently knead the bag to help the milk pass through the ultra-fine mesh. Optionally, the milk can be poured in increments into a strainer lined with 4-layers of cheesecloth placed over a large container. Stir the milk gently with a spoon to help it pass through the cheesecloth. Discard or compost the solids in the bag or cheesecloth.

Now stir in the rejuvelac. Pour into a mason jar or other similar container and cover loosely with a lid. Set aside to culture at room temperature for 24 to 36 hours (culturing will take longer at cooler temperatures and more rapidly during the warmer months). The mixture will separate while culturing; this is normal.

Occasionally tighten the lid and give the mixture a good shake. Be sure to loosen the lid slightly after shaking and continue to culture (loosening the lid will allow the escape of carbon dioxide gas produced during fermentation).

Smell the liquid after 24 hours; the scent of sour milk will indicate that the buttermilk is ready to be refrigerated. Use a clean spoon and taste the mixture. If the milk does not smell or taste sour, continue to culture for an additional 12 hours.

After culturing, tighten the lid and shake thoroughly. Slightly loosen the lid and refrigerate. Chill for 12 hours before using and be sure to retighten the lid before shaking.

Buttermilk Ranch Dressing and Dip

This recipe yields about 1 and ½ cup of tangy and creamy dressing or 1 and ⅓ cup dip.

Ingredients:

- ½ cup Cultured Raw Buttermilk (pg. 34) or Quick Buttermilk (pg. 13) for dressing or ⅓ cup for dip
- 1 cup No-Eggy Mayo (pg. 140)
- 1 tsp Dijon mustard
- ½ tsp onion powder
- ¼ tsp garlic powder
- ¼ tsp fine sea salt or kosher salt, or more to taste
- ¼ tsp coarse ground black pepper, or more to taste
- ¼ tsp vegan Worcestershire sauce
- 1 T finely chopped fresh chives or 1 tsp dried
- 1 T finely chopped fresh parsley or 1 tsp dried
- 1 and ½ tsp finely chopped fresh dill or a ½ tsp dry

Technique:

In a mixing bowl, whisk all the ingredients together except for the herbs until smooth. The ingredients can also be combined in a shaker cup with a tight-fitting lid. Taste and add additional salt or pepper or thin with additional buttermilk to suit your taste. Stir in the herbs and pour into a sealable container (or store in the shaker cup). Refrigerate for a few hours to blend the flavors.

Chilled Cucumber Buttermilk Soup

This deliciously cooling and refreshing raw soup is perfect for serving on a hot summer day. It's also rich in nutrients and probiotics which are beneficial for maintaining a healthy digestive system. This recipe yields about 4 servings.

Ingredients:

- 2 large cucumbers
- ¼ cup diced sweet yellow onion
- 1 quart (4 cups) Cultured Raw Buttermilk (pg. 34)
- sea salt or kosher salt and coarse ground black pepper, to taste
- thinly sliced cucumber rounds, olive oil and minced chives for garnish

Technique:

Thinly slice several cucumber rounds with the peel intact. Set aside for the garnish. Peel the remaining cucumbers, cut in half and scrape out the seeds with a spoon. Chop the cucumbers and add to a blender with the onion, 1 and ½ teaspoon salt and the buttermilk. Process the mixture until smooth.

Pour the mixture into a container and season with black pepper and additional salt to taste. Cover and refrigerate until chilled. To serve, ladle into soup bowls and garnish with the cucumber rounds, minced chives and a drizzle of olive oil.

Cultured Sour Cream

Rich, tangy and velvety smooth, this recipe yields about 2 cups of the finest sour cream. A high-powered blender is recommended for producing the smoothest texture.

Ingredients:

- 1 and ½ cup (7.5 oz by weight) whole raw cashews
- 1 T organic **refined** coconut oil
- ¾ cup Rejuvelac (pg. 30)
- ¼ tsp fine sea salt or kosher salt

Technique:

Soak the cashews for a minimum of 8 hours in the refrigerator with enough filtered or spring water to cover. Drain the cashews, discarding the soaking water, and add them to the blender.

Remove the metal lid from the jar of coconut oil and place the jar in a microwave. Heat just until the solid oil liquefies, about 30 seconds to 1 minute (this will depend upon the solidity of the coconut oil). Alternately, place the jar in about an inch of simmering water and melt the oil in the same manner. Measure 1 tablespoon and add to the blender. Add the rejuvelac and the salt.

Process the contents until completely smooth, stopping to stir or scrape down the sides of blender as necessary. Avoid processing for more than 2 minutes (this can overheat the mixture through friction and potentially harm the culture).

Transfer the mixture to a roomy container with a lid and cover. The cream will develop an "airy" texture and expand during culturing. This is caused by the release of carbon dioxide gas during fermentation and is perfectly normal.

Let the cream culture at room temperature for 24 to 36 hours (warmer weather will accelerate the culturing process, so taste-test after 24 hours for the proper tanginess).

After culturing, stir the sour cream thoroughly. Smooth the surface with the back of a spoon and place a layer of plastic wrap directly in contact with the sour cream. This will discourage the harmless surface discoloration (oxidation) that may occur during extended storage.

Seal the container and place in the refrigerator to chill for 12 hours before using. The sour cream will thicken and continue to develop flavor as it chills.

Cultured Crème Fraîche

Cultured Crème Fraîche has a lighter viscosity and a milder flavor than American-style sour cream. This recipe yields about 2 cups.

To prepare Cultured Crème Fraîche, follow the preceding recipe for Cultured Sour Cream but omit the coconut oil. Culture the cream for 24 hours or until it has reached the desired tanginess.

After culturing, stir the cream thoroughly. Seal the container and place in the refrigerator to chill and thicken for 12 hours before using. The Crème Fraîche will continue to develop flavor as it chills.

Various chopped fresh herbs can be stirred in prior to serving, if desired, to accommodate various ethnic cuisines (cilantro Crème Fraîche, for example, is an excellent topping for Tex-Mex Cuisine).

Greek-Style Yogurt

This recipe produces a thick, creamy, tangy, unflavored and unsweetened yogurt that requires no additional thickening agents such as food starches or gums. So why make your own yogurt? Because most commercial non-dairy yogurts, even the "plain" varieties, have too much sugar added, too many thickening agents added and yet are still too runny to be useful for savory condiments such as Greek Tzatziki and Indian Raita (which require a thick, unsweetened yogurt base). Of course this yogurt can also be sweetened to your liking with organic sugar, natural syrups, fresh fruit or fruit preserves.

The yogurt is made using a blend of whole raw cashews and pure soymilk. The micro-fine solids from the whole raw cashews act as a natural thickener. They also contain the ideal amount of natural sugar (which pure soymilk lacks) to feed the yogurt culture. This combination works synergistically, producing results that cannot be accomplished using soymilk or cashew milk alone.

For consistent results, I recommend using a commercial yogurt maker. Yogurt makers maintain the yogurt at a specific temperature for an extended period of time and are convenient and reasonably affordable. You will also need a candy thermometer or an instant-read thermometer to gauge the proper temperature of the yogurt base as it is warmed on the stove before adding the yogurt culture.

This recipe yields about 5 cups of yogurt. The yogurt can also be cultured using a large slow-cooker (crock pot) and short, pint-size mason jars (canning jars). To do this, fold a cloth kitchen towel in half, and then in half again, and place on the bottom of the slow-cooker. Set the temperature to "warm".

It is important to make sure all your containers and working tools are very clean before you begin so as not to contaminate the yogurt with undesirable bacteria or molds.

Ingredients:

- 1 quart (4 cups) pure soymilk
- 1 cup (5 oz by weight) whole raw cashews
- ½ cup commercial plain soy yogurt* or yogurt from the previous batch; or commercial non-dairy yogurt culture** as directed on the package

*Commercial plain soy yogurt is necessary to get the yogurt started. After that, new batches of yogurt can be started with ½ cup of yogurt from the previous batch. Commercial plain soy yogurt usually contains some sugar, but only a trace amount will be present after blending with the soymilk and cashew mixture. The trace amount of sugar will then become even more dilute when making subsequent batches using yogurt from the previous batch.

When purchasing commercial soy yogurt, be sure the expiration date is not too near, as fresher yogurt will contain more bacterial potency than yogurt that has been stored in market refrigerators for long periods of time. In my experience, commercial almond milk and coconut milk yogurt did not work well as a starter yogurt.

**Commercial non-dairy yogurt culture is packaged and sold in a convenient powdered form and can be purchased from CulturesforHealth.com or BelleandBella.com.

Technique:

When you are ready to begin, remove the glass jars and switch on the power to warm the yogurt maker (or slow-cooker). Rinse the cashews to remove any debris, drain and place them into a blender (they do not require pre-soaking). Add the soymilk and process on high speed for 2 full minutes.

Pour the mixture through a strainer into a 2-quart saucepan. This will capture any larger stray particles; a nut milk bag is not required. If using a candy thermometer, clip it in place in the saucepan, making sure the tip is not touching the metal. Place the saucepan over medium-low heat. Stir slowly and continually until the temperature reaches 100°F. This will only take about 2 minutes. If you're using an instant-read thermometer, check frequently to gauge the temperature while stirring. Remove the saucepan from the heat. Do not exceed 110°F. This is important! If the mixture is too hot, it will destroy the culture. You can also test the mixture by placing a few drops on your wrist; if it's comfortably warm, you're good to go.

Whisk in the yogurt starter until thoroughly blended. Pour the mixture into the yogurt jars. Do not screw the lids on the jars. Set the open jars into the yogurt maker or slow-cooker; put the unit lid in place and culture for 6 to 8 hours. After the 6th hour, taste a spoonful of yogurt. If it is thick and has a nice tang, it is ready. If not, continue to culture for an additional hour or more. If the yogurt is not tangy after the 8th hour, the yogurt starter was not viable.

After culturing, screw the lids on the jars and refrigerate for a minimum of 12 hours. This will further develop the flavor. While refrigerating, a small amount of liquid, or whey, may collect on the sides and bottom of the jars. This is normal. Consume the yogurt within 3 weeks (because this is a cultured food, it may stay fresh longer, but 3 weeks is a rough guideline). Be sure to reserve ½ cup for starting your next batch.

Greek Tzatziki

Greek Tzatziki is a cucumber sauce used as a condiment for Greek and other Mediterranean cuisine and can be made with either Greek-Style Yogurt or Cultured Sour Cream. This recipe yields about 2 cups.

Ingredients:

- 1 small cucumber, peeled or unpeeled, seeded and diced
- 1 cup Greek-Style Yogurt (pg. 38) or Cultured Sour Cream (pg. 37)
- 2 T olive oil
- ¼ cup finely minced shallot or red onion
- 2 cloves garlic, finely minced
- 2 tsp red wine vinegar or raw apple cider vinegar
- ½ tsp fine sea salt or kosher salt, or more to taste
- ¼ tsp coarse ground black pepper, or more to taste
- 1 tsp chopped fresh dill (optional)

Technique:

Wrap the diced cucumber in a few layers of paper towels or a lint-free kitchen towel and squeeze to remove the excess moisture. Add the cucumbers and the remaining ingredients to the yogurt or sour cream and stir until blended. Season the sauce with additional salt or pepper to taste. Chill for a minimum of two hours to blend the flavors. Garnish with the chopped fresh dill just before serving.

Indian Raita

Raita is an Indian, Pakistani and Bangladeshi condiment used to temper the heat of Indian spices and can be made with either Greek-Style Yogurt or Cultured Sour Cream. This recipe yields about 2 cups.

Ingredients:

- 1 small cucumber, peeled or unpeeled, seeded and diced
- 1 cup Greek-Style Yogurt (pg. 38) or Cultured Sour Cream (pg. 37)
- 2 T olive oil
- ¼ cup finely chopped green onions, including the green tops
- 2 tsp fresh lemon juice
- ½ tsp fine sea salt or kosher salt, or more to taste
- ¼ tsp ground cumin
- 1 T chopped fresh mint (optional)

Technique:

Wrap the diced cucumber in a few layers of paper towels or a lint-free kitchen towel and squeeze to remove the excess moisture. Add the cucumber and the remaining ingredients to the yogurt or sour cream and stir until blended. Season the sauce with additional salt and cumin to taste. Chill for a minimum of two hours to blend the flavors. Garnish with a sprig of fresh mint just before serving.

Mango Lassi

Mango Lassi is an Indian beverage made from yogurt and the pulp from fresh or frozen mangoes. It's wonderful for cooling the heat of spicy Indian cuisine.

Ingredients:

- 2 ripe, sweet mangos
- 1 and ½ cups Greek-Style Yogurt (pg. 38) or commercial plain non-dairy yogurt
- organic sugar or other natural sweetener, to taste
- 2 cups crushed ice

Technique:

Peel and dice the mango and add to the blender. Add the rest of the ingredients and purée until smooth and frothy. Serve immediately.

An Introduction to Non-Dairy Cheeses

While commercial non-dairy cheeses have made vast improvements since they were first marketed many years ago, I feel that most of them still lack something in flavor and/or texture. Over the past several years, I have researched the properties of dairy cheese and experimented with various plant-based ingredients to create cheeses that simulate their dairy counterparts as closely as possible.

Dairy cheese is comprised of proteins and fat from milk, usually the milk of cows, buffalo, goats, or sheep. It is produced by coagulation of the milk protein *casein*. Typically, the milk is acidified and the addition of the enzyme *rennet* (derived from the stomachs of cows, goats and sheep) causes coagulation. The solids are then separated and pressed into final form. For a few cheeses, such as mascarpone and paneer, the milk is curdled by adding acids such as vinegar or lemon juice.

Most dairy cheeses are acidified by bacteria, which turns lactose (milk sugar) into lactic acid, with the addition of rennet completing the curdling process. At this stage, the cheese is considered fresh or unripened. Varieties that fall into this category include cottage cheese, cream cheese and ricotta.

Other varieties are ripened by the addition of various strains of bacteria and fungi/molds and then aged for varying periods of time. Ripened cheeses are further classified by texture or aging process.

However, non-dairy cheeses need to be produced using completely different processes since plant milks do not contain casein and since rennet is not used (and would not be used for ethical reasons) as a coagulant. Vegetarian rennet does exist (enzymes derived from various microbial and plant sources), but it only works with animal milk.

In this book, several techniques are used to produce a wide variety of non-dairy cheeses according to different criteria: cultured and uncultured; melting ability; textures ranging from soft and spreadable to firm and solid; and varying degrees of sharpness.

Sharpness is best described as a complex, tangy and/or pungent flavor. Cheddars and blues are the most common cheeses described as sharp, although others are sometimes grouped this way as well. While the method of production dictates a cheese's sharpness, ultimately it is simply a measure used to categorize the flavor of the cheese.

The degree of sharpness in dairy cheddar cheese, for example, is determined by the breakdown of fats and proteins by bacteria and enzymes during aging. In other words, the longer the cheddar ages, the sharper it gets (9 months minimum for sharp cheddars and 15 months minimum for extra-sharp). This process produces compounds (*aldehydes*, *alpha-keto acids* and *esters*) that give the cheddar its characteristic sharp and pungent flavor.

For the cultured cheeses in this cookbook, complex sharp and extra-sharp flavors are produced by brief periods of lacto-bacterial fermentation (very brief when compared to dairy cheeses). In some cases, other natural ingredients are added to help develop pungency during "ripening".

For the uncultured cheeses in this cookbook, varying degrees of sharpness and pungency are created by introducing combinations of acids (commercial lactic acid or lemon juice and/or vinegar) with other natural ingredients.

Both processes are much less complicated than dairy cheese production and more instantly gratifying (although a little more patience is required for the cultured cheeses).

Please note that ingredients such as onion powder, dry ground mustard and garlic powder are not intended to impart an onion, mustard or garlic flavor, but rather to impart pungent undertones that are present in ripened dairy cheeses. Measurements of these ingredients are based upon my personal preference and taste. If you absolutely abhor the flavor of mustard, then don't add mustard when preparing the cheeses. This is just common sense. If you're particularly sensitive to the flavor of onion powder, then decrease or omit the onion powder. Mixtures should be tasted and salt added to your preference. The formulas are basic guidelines and seasonings can be adjusted, within reason, to accommodate personal preferences.

Many varieties of cheese are inherently mild, whether they're dairy or non-dairy, so don't expect non-dairy mozzarella, for example, to be bursting with flavor. Dairy mozzarella isn't bursting with flavor either. Some cheeses are better for cooking; others are ideal for snacking. Many of the cheese formulas are very similar to each other, with only subtle ingredient variations. The cultured cream cheese formula, for example, is nearly identical to the chèvre formula, with the moisture content and the length of time culturing being the only difference. The same is true with many dairy cheeses.

Please keep in mind that the cheeses were formulated based upon my memory of dairy cheese flavors and textures. It's been a long time since I've consumed dairy cheeses, so my memory is vague at best. Also keep in mind that the cheeses are prepared in a completely different way, and with different ingredients than dairy cheeses, so accurate flavors and textures can only be replicated to a certain degree. If you curb your expectation of creating an exact dairy reproduction, then the non-dairy cheeses should sufficiently satisfy your desire for cheese flavors and textures.

Cultured Cashew-Based Cheeses

The cultured cashew-based cheeses derive their tangy flavor, or sharpness, from actual culturing (fermentation) with "friendly" bacteria, rather than through the use of commercial lactic acid and fruit acids such as vinegar and lemon juice. A thick cream base created from raw cashews is used as the medium for culturing and rejuvelac is used as the culturing agent. So why use cashews and not other nuts? Cashews, unlike other oily tree nuts, contain up to 10% of their weight in starch. This starch, which is comprised of a chain of glucose units, makes cashews a more effective medium for culturing than other nuts, which in turn makes them ideal for creating the finest cultured cheeses. Simply stated: cashews work.

The cashew cream base is prepared by grinding raw cashews that have been soaked in water until hydrated. This creates an entirely different composition than cashew butter which is prepared by grinding raw or roasted cashews (however, dry grinding raw cashews is used for creating Hard Parmesan, pg. 97).

The degree of sharpness is determined by the period of time the cheese is cultured at room temperature, usually from 1 to 3 days, depending on the variety of cheese and the ambient temperature. During this time, the lactobacillus bacteria convert the natural starch/sugar in the cashew cream into lactic acid, which provides the tangy flavor. In some cases, mellow white miso paste is added as a secondary culturing agent, which enhances the flavor of the cheese as it ferments and then ripens. Other natural ingredients may be used to impart unique and complex flavor characteristics to the cheese.

Because the cheeses contain live cultures, seaweed derivatives such as carrageenan and agar are not used as firming agents, since both require heat for activation. Instead, refined coconut oil is used as a firming agent because of its tendency to harden when chilled. The amount of coconut oil used in the formulas determines the finished texture, ranging from soft and spreadable to firm and somewhat crumbly. The coconut oil also provides the fat necessary to produce the proper "melt-in-your-mouth" quality to the cheeses. However, while the cultured cheeses will soften or dissolve when exposed to heat, they will not melt in the same manner as the Block and Wheel Cheeses and they definitely will not stretch.

A food processor is recommended and a high-powered blender is essential for efficient processing. Since processing foods in a high-powered blender can generate a great deal of heat through friction, the food processor is used first to break the cashews down into a coarse paste. By initially breaking down the cashews into a coarse paste, the running time on the blender is then reduced, which ensures that the bacterial culture is not destroyed by excessive exposure to heat. The high-powered blender then processes the cashew paste into the smoothest texture possible, which is something the food processor cannot do alone. Avoid using a standard blender for these recipes if possible, as you will quickly burn out the motor!

Cultured cheeses such as chèvre are produced in somewhat larger portions (about 12 oz) than you might normally purchase of their dairy counterparts (typically 4 to 8 oz). This is because a larger volume of material is easier to process in the blender and inevitably a small amount of product that cannot be retrieved from under the blender blades will be lost. However, since the cheeses are cultured, they can be refrigerated for several weeks and you won't have to prepare them as often.

Cream Cheese

This recipe produces the finest, cultured non-dairy cream cheese. A food processor is recommended for initially breaking down the cashews and a high-powered blender is essential for the smoothest finished texture. This recipe yields about 12 ounces.

Ingredients:

- 1 and ½ cups (7.5 oz by weight) whole raw cashews
- ¼ cup organic **refined** coconut oil
- ½ tsp fine sea salt or kosher salt
- ⅓ cup Rejuvelac (pg. 30)

Technique:

Soak the cashews for a minimum of 8 hours in the refrigerator with enough filtered or spring water to cover. Drain the cashews, discarding the soaking water, and add them to a food processor.

Remove the metal lid from the jar of coconut oil and place the jar in a microwave. Heat just until the solid oil liquefies, about 30 seconds to 1 minute (this will depend upon the solidity of the coconut oil). Alternately, place the jar in about an inch of simmering water and melt the oil in the same manner. Measure ¼ cup and add to the food processor with the salt. Process the contents into a paste, about 2 minutes.

Transfer the cashew paste to the blender; add the rejuvelac and process on high speed until completely smooth. The mixture will be very thick, so stop to scrape down the sides of the blender and push the mixture down into the blades as necessary. Use a tamper tool if provided with your blender to keep the mixture turning in the blades. Avoid continual processing for more than 2 minutes, as this can overheat the mixture through friction and potentially harm the culture.

Transfer the mixture to a clean, roomy container with a lid. Cover and let the cheese culture at room temperature for 24 hours. The cream cheese mixture will expand and develop an "airy" texture during culturing. This is caused by the release of carbon dioxide gas during fermentation and is perfectly normal.

After culturing, stir the cream cheese thoroughly. Smooth the surface with the back of a spoon and place a layer of plastic wrap directly in contact with the cheese. This will discourage the harmless surface discoloration that may occur during extended storage. Now seal the container and place in the refrigerator to chill for 12 hours before using. The cream cheese will continue to develop flavor as it chills.

Variations: For cream cheese with onion and chives, stir in 1 tablespoon dried minced onion and 1 tablespoon freeze-dried minced chives **before** chilling. For fruit flavored cream cheese, mix ¼ cup all-fruit jam into the cream cheese **after** it has chilled and firmed.

Chèvre

Chèvre (from the French word for "goat"), is a semi-soft cheese traditionally made from the milk of goats. Non-dairy chèvre is a cultured cashew-based cheese with a tangy, refreshing flavor - no goats involved!

Chèvre also serves as a wonderful cheese base for rolling in various dried or fresh herbs, spices, crushed raw or toasted nuts and seeds, or swirled with various wine, vinegar or fruit syrup reductions to create unique variations of flavor. A food processor is recommended for initially breaking down the cashews and a high-powered blender is essential for the smoothest finished texture. Chèvre is typically packaged in small portions of 4 to 6 ounces. This recipe yields two 6 ounce portions.

Ingredients:

- 1 and ½ cup (7.5 oz by weight) whole raw cashews
- ¼ cup organic **refined** coconut oil
- 1 tsp fine sea salt or kosher salt
- ¼ cup Rejuvelac (pg. 30)

Technique:

Soak the cashews for a minimum of 8 hours in the refrigerator with enough filtered or spring water to cover. Drain the cashews, discarding the water, and add them to a food processor.

Remove the metal lid from the jar of coconut oil and place the jar in a microwave. Heat just until the solid oil liquefies, about 30 seconds to 1 minute (this will depend upon the solidity of the coconut oil). Alternately, place the jar in about an inch of simmering water and melt the oil in the same manner. Measure ¼ cup and add to the food processor with the salt. Process the contents into a paste, about 2 minutes.

Transfer the cashew paste to a high-powered blender; add the rejuvelac and process on high speed until completely smooth. The mixture will be very thick, so stop to scrape down the sides of the blender and push the mixture down into the blades as necessary. Use a tamper tool if provided with your blender to keep the mixture turning in the blades. Avoid continual processing for more than 2 minutes, as this can overheat the mixture through friction and potentially harm the culture.

Transfer the cheese mixture to a clean container with a lid (be sure to use a container with extra room, as the mixture will expand when culturing due to the release of carbon dioxide gas). Cover and let the cheese culture at room temperature for 48 hours (warmer weather will accelerate the culturing process, so taste-test after 36 hours). For a tangier chèvre, let the cheese culture for up to 72 hours.

After culturing, stir the cheese mixture until creamy, cover and place the container in the refrigerator to chill for 24 hours until the cheese is very firm.

After firming the cheese, lay out a sheet of plastic wrap. Scoop up half of the cheese mixture from the container and place on the wrap. With your fingers, form the mixture into a small log shape (keep a moist towel nearby to wipe your hands). Don't worry about shaping perfection, as the wrap will shape the log for you when rolled.

Roll the cheese log in the wrap, twist the ends tightly and place the cheese in the refrigerator for a minimum of 48 hours to fully ripen. Repeat the procedure with the remaining portion of cheese. To serve, simply remove the wrap and place on a serving plate.

Peppercorn Chèvre

For this variation, the cultured chèvre is rolled in cracked black peppercorns or a rainbow blend of cracked mixed peppercorns.

This recipe yields two 6 ounce portions; however, the second portion of cheese can be seasoned differently, if desired.

Technique:

First, prepare the chèvre; culture and refrigerate until firm as instructed on page 46.

After firming the cheese, lay out a sheet of plastic wrap. Sprinkle the wrap with 1 teaspoon of cracked pepper. Scoop up half of the cheese mixture from the container and place on the pepper. With your fingers, form the mixture into a small log shape (keep a moist towel nearby to wipe your hands). Don't worry about shaping perfection, as the wrap will shape the log for you when rolled. Sprinkle with an additional teaspoon of cracked pepper and press the pepper into the cheese with your fingers.

Roll the cheese log in the wrap, twist the ends tightly and place the cheese in the refrigerator for a minimum of 48 hours to fully ripen. Repeat the procedure with the remaining portion of cheese or reserve for flavoring with different seasonings. To serve, simply remove the wrap and place on a serving plate.

Chèvre with Fines Herbes

In French cooking, the term *fines herbes* refers to a blend of parsley, chives, chervil and tarragon. For this variation, the cultured chèvre is rolled in dried fines herbes.

Fines herbes can be found in most supermarkets in the dried spice and herb aisle. Fresh herbs can also be used, although I recommend rolling the cheese in the herbs just before serving since their moisture content might affect the cheese when stored.

This recipe yields two 6 ounce portions; however, the second portion of cheese can be seasoned differently, if desired.

Technique:

First, prepare the chèvre; culture and refrigerate until firm as instructed on page 46.

After firming the cheese, lay out a sheet of plastic wrap. Sprinkle the wrap with 1 teaspoon of dried fine herbes. Scoop up half of the cheese mixture from the container and place on the herbs. With your fingers, form the mixture into a small log shape (keep a moist towel nearby to wipe your hands). Don't worry about shaping perfection as the wrap will shape the log for you when rolled. Sprinkle with an additional teaspoon of herbs and press the herbs into the cheese with your fingers.

Roll the cheese log in the wrap, twist the ends tightly and place the cheese in the refrigerator for a minimum of 48 hours to fully ripen. Repeat the procedure with the remaining portion of cheese or reserve for flavoring with different seasonings. To serve, simply remove the wrap and place on a serving plate.

Chèvre with Mulled Wine Swirl

This unique holiday dessert cheese is laced with a sweet, syrupy reduction of red wine infused with the flavors of orange, cinnamon and clove. Only a small amount of reduction is needed; any remaining reduction, also known as a *gastrique*, is wonderful for drizzling over fresh fruit. This recipe yields two 6 ounce portions; however, the second portion of cheese can be flavored differently, if desired.

For the mulled wine reduction, you will need:

- ½ cup red wine, any variety
- 1 T organic sugar
- 1-inch piece of orange peel
- 1-inch piece of cinnamon stick
- 5 whole cloves

Technique:

First, prepare the chèvre; culture and refrigerate until firm as instructed on page 46.

In a small saucepan, stir together the wine, sugar and spices over medium-low heat. Simmer to reduce the volume by half, about 5 minutes. Let cool completely. When cooled, the reduction will become very syrupy.

Lay out a sheet of plastic wrap. Scoop up half of the cheese mixture and place on the wrap. With the back of a spoon, press the cheese into a flattened square about ½-inch thick and drizzle 2 teaspoons of the reduction over the cheese. Use the edge of the wrap to help lift and fold the cheese over to get the roll started. With the help of the plastic wrap, continue rolling the cheese into a log. After the roll is complete, use your fingers to compress and compact the log shape. Don't worry about perfection; the plastic wrap will do the final shaping for you.

Now roll the cheese log in the wrap itself, twist the ends tightly and place the cheese in the refrigerator for a minimum of 48 hours to fully ripen. Repeat the procedure with the remaining portion of cheese or reserve for flavoring differently. To serve, simply remove the wrap and place on a serving plate.

Chèvre with Rosemary Balsamic Swirl

This delightful dessert cheese is laced with a sweet, syrupy reduction of dark balsamic vinegar infused with the flavor of fresh rosemary. Only a small amount of reduction is needed; any remaining reduction, also known as a *gastrique*, is wonderful for drizzling over fresh fruit. This recipe yields two 6 ounce portions; however, the second portion of cheese can be flavored differently, if desired.

For the rosemary balsamic reduction, you will need:

- ½ cup dark balsamic vinegar
- 1 T organic sugar
- 1 small sprig of fresh rosemary

Technique:

First, prepare the chèvre; culture and refrigerate until firm as instructed on page 46.

In a small saucepan, stir together the vinegar, sugar and rosemary over medium-low heat. Simmer to reduce the volume by half, about 5 minutes. Let cool completely. When cooled, the reduction will become very syrupy.

Lay out a sheet of plastic wrap. Scoop up half of the cheese mixture and place on the wrap. With the back of a spoon, press the cheese into a flattened square about ½-inch thick and drizzle 2 teaspoons of the reduction over the cheese. Use the edge of the wrap to help lift and fold the cheese over to get the roll started. With the help of the plastic wrap, continue rolling the cheese into a log. After the roll is complete, use your fingers to compress and compact the log shape. Don't worry about perfection; the plastic wrap will do the final shaping for you.

Now roll the cheese log in the wrap itself, twist the ends tightly and place the cheese in the refrigerator for a minimum of 48 hours to fully ripen. Repeat the procedure with the remaining portion of cheese or reserve for flavoring differently. To serve, simply remove the wrap and place on a serving plate.

White Cheddar Amandine

White Cheddar Amandine is a semi-soft, almond-encrusted cheese log with a sharp cheddar flavor that continues to develop and intensify as it ages. If preferred, the cheese mixture can be divided in half and shaped into two 6-ounce cheese balls. A food processor is recommended for initially breaking down the cashews and a high-powered blender is essential for the smoothest finished texture. This recipe yields about 12 ounces.

Ingredients:

- 1 and ½ cups (7.5 oz by weight) whole raw cashews
- ⅓ cup organic **refined** coconut oil
- 2 T nutritional yeast flakes
- 2 T mellow white miso paste
- ¾ tsp onion powder
- ½ tsp dry ground mustard
- ½ tsp fine sea salt or kosher salt
- ¼ cup Rejuvelac (pg. 30)

For the crust, you will need:

- ⅓ cup slivered raw almonds

Technique:

Soak the cashews for a minimum of 8 hours in the refrigerator with enough filtered or spring water to cover. Drain the cashews, discarding the soaking water, and add them to a food processor.

Remove the metal lid from the jar of coconut oil and place the jar in a microwave. Heat just until the solid oil liquefies, about 30 seconds to 1 minute (this will depend upon the solidity of the coconut oil). Alternately, place the jar in about an inch of simmering water and melt the oil in the same manner. Measure ⅓ cup and add to the food processor. Add the nutritional yeast, miso, onion powder, dry mustard and salt. Process the contents into a paste, about 2 minutes.

Transfer the seasoned cashew paste to the blender, add the rejuvelac and process on high speed until completely smooth. The mixture will be very thick, so stop to scrape down the sides of the blender and push the mixture down into the blades as necessary. Use a tamper tool if provided with your blender to keep the mixture turning in the blades. Avoid continual processing for more than 2 minutes, as this can overheat the mixture through friction and potentially harm the culture.

Transfer the mixture to a clean container with a lid. Cover and let the cheese culture at room temperature for 48 to 72 hours (warmer weather will accelerate the culturing process, so taste-test after 36 hours for the proper sharpness). The cheese will develop an "airy" texture during culturing. This is caused by the release of carbon dioxide gas during fermentation and is perfectly normal.

After culturing, stir the cheese mixture until creamy, cover and place the container in the refrigerator to chill for 12 hours until the cheese is firm. After the cheese has chilled and firmed, place the slivered almonds into a food processor and pulse until coarsely ground. Add the ground almonds to a dry skillet and place over medium heat. Stir frequently until the almonds are toasted and are emitting a very nutty aroma. Be careful not let them burn! Scatter the ground toasted almonds on a plate and allow them to cool before proceeding.

Lay out a sheet of plastic wrap on a work surface and set aside. Next, scoop up the cheese mixture and with your hands, form the mixture into a log shape. Don't worry about perfection; the wrap will shape the log when rolled. Roll the log in the ground nuts on the plate, gently pressing the nuts into the cheese with your fingers.

Place the log on the wrap and roll the cheese inside the wrap; twist the ends tightly. Place back in the refrigerator for 72 hours to ripen. To serve, simply remove the wrap and place on a serving plate.

Extra-Sharp White Cheddar

Extra-Sharp White Cheddar is a semi-firm cheese with an extra-sharp cheddar flavor that continues to develop and intensify as it ages. It's sure to please the most discerning sharp cheddar connoisseur. A food processor is recommended for initially breaking down the cashews and a high-powered blender is essential for the smoothest finished texture. This recipe yields about 12 ounces.

Ingredients:

- 1 and ½ cups (7.5 oz by weight) whole raw cashews
- ½ cup organic **refined** coconut oil
- 2 T nutritional yeast flakes
- 2 T mellow white miso paste
- 1 tsp onion powder
- ¾ tsp dry ground mustard
- ½ tsp fine sea salt or kosher salt
- ¼ cup Rejuvelac (pg. 30)

Technique:

Soak the cashews for a minimum of 8 hours in the refrigerator with enough filtered or spring water to cover. Drain the cashews, discarding the soaking water, and add them to a food processor.

Remove the metal lid from the jar of coconut oil and place the jar in a microwave. Heat just until the solid oil liquefies, about 30 seconds to 1 minute (this will depend upon the solidity of the coconut oil). Alternately, place the jar in about an inch of simmering water and melt the oil in the same manner. Measure ½ cup and add to the food processor. Add the nutritional yeast, miso, onion powder, dry mustard and salt to the food processor. Process the contents into a paste, about 2 minutes.

Transfer the seasoned cashew paste to the blender, add the rejuvelac and process on high speed until completely smooth. The mixture will be very thick, so stop to scrape down the sides of the blender and push the mixture down into the blades as necessary. Use a tamper tool if provided with your blender to keep the mixture turning in the blades. Avoid continual processing for more than 2 minutes, as this can overheat the mixture through friction and potentially harm the culture.

Transfer the mixture to a clean container with a lid, cover and let the cheese culture at room temperature for 72 hours (warmer weather will accelerate the culturing process, so taste-test after 48 hours for the proper sharpness). The cheese will develop an "airy" texture during culturing. This is caused by the release of carbon dioxide gas during fermentation and is perfectly normal.

After culturing, line a round, square or rectangular container that will hold a minimum of 2 cups liquid with plastic wrap. Be sure to leave excess wrap hanging over the sides. The container will serve as a form to shape the cheese and the plastic wrap will help lift the cheese from the container after firming.

Stir the cheese until creamy and then transfer to the prepared form. Press the cheese mixture thoroughly into the form and smooth the surface with the back of a spoon as best you can. Cover and place the container in the refrigerator for 72 hours to firm and ripen.

To serve, simply lift the cheese from the form, remove the plastic wrap and slice as needed. Keep the cheese stored in the refrigerator wrapped tightly in plastic or in a zip-lock bag. The cheese will continue to develop flavor and become somewhat crumbly as it ages.

Bleu Cheese

Dairy blue cheese has a very distinct, pungent aroma and flavor created by the mold *Penicillium roqueforti,* as well as by specially cultivated bacteria. This mold is also responsible for the blue-green "veins" within the cheese.

Admittedly, mimicking the flavor and appearance of blue cheese with plant-based ingredients available to the home vegan cook was a bit of a challenge. Although it lacks some of the pungency of dairy blue cheese normally created by the *Penicillium* mold, it has a sharp, tangy flavor, a semi-firm crumbly texture and the characteristic blue-green "veins" that give bleu cheese its name. A food processor and a high-powered blender are recommended for efficient processing. This recipe yields about 12 ounces.

Ingredients:

- 1 and ½ cup (7.5 oz by weight) whole raw cashews
- ½ cup organic **refined** coconut oil
- 1 T mellow white miso paste
- 1 and ¼ tsp fine sea salt or kosher salt
- ½ tsp onion powder
- ¼ tsp garlic powder
- ¼ cup Rejuvelac (pg. 30)
- ¼ tsp blue-green algae powder (spirulina)

Technique:

Soak the cashews for a minimum of 8 hours in the refrigerator with enough filtered or spring water to cover. Drain the cashews, discarding the soaking water and add them to a food processor.

Remove the metal lid from the jar of coconut oil and place the jar in a microwave. Heat just until the solid oil liquefies, about 30 seconds to 1 minute (this will depend upon the solidity of the coconut oil). Alternately, place the jar in about an inch of simmering water and melt the oil in the same manner. Measure ½ cup and add to the food processor. Add the miso, salt, onion powder and garlic powder to the food processor. Process the contents into a paste, about 2 minutes.

Transfer the seasoned cashew paste to the blender, add the rejuvelac and process on high speed until completely smooth. The mixture will be very thick, so stop to scrape down the sides of the blender and push the mixture down into the blades as necessary. Use a tamper tool if provided with your blender to keep the mixture turning in the blades. Avoid continual processing for more than 2 minutes, as this can overheat the mixture through friction and potentially harm the culture.

Transfer the mixture to a clean container with a lid, cover and let the cheese culture at room temperature for 48 to 72 hours (warmer weather will accelerate the culturing process, so taste-test after 48 hours for the proper sharpness). The cheese will develop an "airy" texture during culturing. This is caused by the release of carbon dioxide gas during fermentation and is perfectly normal.

After culturing, remove the lid and stir the cheese until creamy and then dot the surface of the cheese in several places with the algae powder. Now fold (rather than stir) the cheese over a few times to create swirls of blue-green color. Scoop the cheese into another clean container lined with plastic wrap. The plastic wrap will help lift the cheese from the form after chilling and ripening. Pack the cheese into the container and smooth the surface with the back of a spoon. Cover with a lid or plastic wrap and refrigerate for 72 hours.

After 72 hours, lift the cheese from the form and remove the plastic wrap. The cheese is now ready to slice or crumble as needed. Store tightly wrapped in plastic wrap or a zip-lock bag. The cheese will become firmer, more crumbly and the flavor will continue to develop as the cheese ages. Do not freeze.

Chunky Bleu Cheese Dressing

This incredible non-dairy dressing tastes remarkably like restaurant-style dairy blue cheese dressing. This dressing is also excellent when served as a dip for crudités (assorted sliced raw vegetables).

Ingredients:

- 4 oz Bleu Cheese (pg. 52) or Gorgonzola (pg. 88)
- 1 cup No-Eggy Mayo (pg. 140)
- 3 T Cultured Sour Cream (pg. 37)
- 2 T plain unsweetened non-dairy milk, or more to adjust consistency
- ¼ tsp coarse ground black pepper, or more to taste
- ¼ tsp fine sea salt or kosher salt, or more to taste
- ¼ tsp vegan Worcestershire Sauce

Technique:

Add ½ of the crumbled bleu cheese and the remaining ingredients to a food processor or blender and process the contents until smooth. If you wish to thin the consistency, add small amounts of non-dairy milk until the desired consistency is achieved; season with additional salt and pepper to taste. Transfer to a covered container and stir in the remaining crumbled bleu cheese. Seal the container and refrigerate until chilled before using.

Iceberg Wedge Salad
with Chunky Bleu Cheese Dressing

Crisp iceberg lettuce wedges are dressed with a cool and tangy cultured bleu cheese dressing and then garnished with diced tomatoes, crispy crumbled vegan bacon and additional bleu cheese crumbles.

Ingredients:

- 1 head iceberg lettuce
- Chunky Bleu Cheese Dressing (pg. 53)
- 1 vine-ripened tomato or several cherry or grape tomatoes, diced
- ½ cup crumbled Bleu Cheese (pg. 52)
- 1 cup cooked and crumbled vegan bacon
- coarse ground black pepper, to taste

Technique:

Remove any loose or torn outer leaves from a head of iceberg lettuce. Cut the head into quarters, cutting from the stem end to the top of the head. Remove the tough core from each quarter but leave enough to hold the wedge together. On each salad plate, place 1 wedge of lettuce. Drizzle bleu cheese dressing over the wedge and garnish with tomatoes, crumbled bleu cheese, crumbled vegan bacon and coarse ground black pepper, to taste.

Block and Wheel Cheeses
An Introduction

One of my greatest challenges as a plant-based food science enthusiast and chef was to produce non-dairy cheeses that resemble their dairy counterparts in terms of flavor, texture and melting ability. After experimenting extensively with various plant-based ingredients in different combinations and ratios, I was finally successful at producing cheeses that satisfied my criteria.

The Block and Wheel Cheeses can best be described as "instant" cheeses. This means that they do not require culturing or ripening, but rather obtain their flavor from the introduction of commercial lactic acid and/or fruit acids, often with the addition of other natural flavoring ingredients.

The Block and Wheel Cheeses are created through a process known as emulsification. Simply stated, emulsification is the process where two or more ingredients that wouldn't normally mix together, such as oil and non-dairy milk, are blended together into a homogenous mixture.

The cheeses were formulated using pure soymilk, therefore pure soymilk is recommended for achieving the best results. Homemade almond milk, when prepared according to the recipe in this cookbook, can also be used successfully for preparing the cheeses.

Homemade raw cashew milk can potentially be used as an alternate to soymilk or almond milk; however due to the composition of raw cashew milk, heat and stirring alone will not successfully emulsify the milk with the oil and an immersion blender is required to force emulsification while the cheese is being cooked. This can be a little tricky until you have become proficient at preparing the cheeses using soymilk or almond milk. It should be noted that processing with an immersion blender is unsuitable for any cheeses containing special ingredients, such as sautéed jalapeno, red pepper flakes, dried minced onion, etc., because blending will pulverize such ingredients.

Due to their watery consistency and abundance of additives, commercial nut milks, rice milk, oat milk, hemp milk and coconut milk beverage are not recommended for preparing the cheeses.

Soymilk Base

Soymilk is a stable emulsion (meaning it does not separate like other plant milks) and is the closest to dairy milk in terms of complete protein, carbohydrate and fat composition. It emulsifies easily and successfully with oil simply by heating and vigorous stirring, and produces textures remarkably similar to dairy cheese. Soymilk also reacts to the acids in the cheese formulas, which contributes to the finished texture. "Pure" refers to the lack of sweeteners and thickening additives which are often used in commercial soymilk.

The Block and Wheel Cheeses are sensitive to thickening additives which are commonly found in most commercial brands of soymilk; therefore, pure soymilk is recommended for preparing the cheeses. Lambda carrageenan is the most common additive found in commercial soymilk. Lambda carrageenan is a cold soluble, non-gelling form of carrageenan used to thicken commercial dairy and non-dairy products. It is very different in composition than kappa carrageenan, which is the heat-activated seaweed derivative used to firm the Block and Wheel Cheeses.

Thickeners such as lambda carrageenan will increase the viscosity of the cheese mixture as it cooks, making it thick and "sludgy" and much more difficult to stir. After repeated testing and sampling, I found that the finished cheese had a peculiar, rubbery texture. Vitamin and calcium fortification, however, will not affect the cooking process or finished texture of the cheeses.

Westsoy™ in the United States produces pure soymilk which is ideal for the preparing the cheeses. Homemade soymilk is an option for those who wish to prepare their own soymilk or if pure commercial soymilk is unavailable. I recommend following the Soymilk recipe on page 12, to be sure the soymilk has the proper consistency for preparing the cheeses. If the soymilk is too watery, it will not yield a creamy finished texture.

Almond Milk Base

Homemade almond milk, when prepared according to the recipe in this cookbook (Almond Milk, pg. 17), can be used successfully for preparing the Block and Wheel Cheeses. This is especially useful for individuals who are allergic to soy. However, almond milk is not stable like soymilk, and the risk of a broken emulsion is greater if the cooking temperature is too high and the mixture is heated too quickly. Please follow the instructions carefully to prevent this from occurring while cooking the cheese mixtures.

The almond milk recipe in this cookbook is formulated to produce the proper consistency for preparing the Block and Wheel Cheeses. Commercial almond milk is not recommended as it is too watery for cheese making, contains too many additives, and will not produce the proper creamy texture in the finished cheeses.

It's true that homemade almond milk is more expensive to prepare, but there's a reason why commercial almond milk is so affordable: In order to keep the price low for the consumer, almond milk manufacturers use a very small amount of almonds for each quart of milk. A weak suspension of water and almonds is created and then a variety of ingredients are added to make it palatable. Sweeteners are sometimes added and lecithin is added to homogenize the milk. Food gum, starch and lambda carrageenan are added to thicken and stabilize the milk. Not only is the milk still too watery for cheese making purposes, but the additives can wreak havoc with the cooking process and finished texture of the cheese.

This same watery constitution and abundance of additives also applies to other commercial nut milks, rice milk, oat milk, hemp milk and coconut milk beverage. If you still choose to experiment, be aware that this may result in a broken emulsion, or finished textures that are very different than the cheeses prepared with pure soymilk or homemade almond milk. I hope I've made my point.

Refined coconut oil provides the necessary fat which transforms the soymilk or almond milk and other ingredients into cheese. Without the fat, the mixture would simply be a gelled block of flavored non-dairy milk and it will not have the firmness, texture, mouthfeel or melting ability of real cheese. The coconut oil also contributes to the firmness of the cheese, since it solidifies when chilled, and enables the cheese to melt evenly when exposed to heat.

Avoid virgin coconut oil for cheese making, as it will impart an undesirable coconut flavor. Refined coconut oil can only be substituted with sustainably-sourced palm oil or organic de-scented cocoa butter.

Tapioca flour, also known as tapioca starch, is used as a thickening agent. It also provides a degree of "stretch" when the cheeses are melted. Other starches will not work in the same manner, so there is no exact substitute. If you absolutely must substitute, use arrowroot powder.

Kappa carrageenan, a derivative of seaweed, is used as a firming agent because of its heat-reversible properties. "Heat-reversible" refers to it ability to re-melt when exposed to heat after it has already been set (unlike agar, which is not heat-reversible).

Agar cannot be used as a substitute for carrageenan in these recipes because 1) it is not heat-reversible; 2) it requires excessively large amounts to achieve the same firming effect as carrageenan; and 3) it needs to be dissolved in simmering water in order to activate and gel properly.

Kappa carrageenan is derived from a species of seaweed called *Kappaphycus alvarezii*. This is very different than powdered Irish Moss (*Chondrus crispus*) which contains about 55% carrageenan. Irish moss is commonly used as a clarifying agent in the process of brewing beer, particularly in home brewing.

So no, powdered Irish Moss will not work for these cheeses, nor will iota carrageenan which forms softer gels.

Kappa carrageenan is sensitive to acids. As the pH is lowered, hydrolysis of the carrageenan polymer occurs, resulting in loss of viscosity and gelling capability. In other words, as acids increase (or the pH decreases), kappa carrageenan loses its firming power. This limits the Block and Wheel Cheeses to only mild degrees of acidity (and thus sharpness). Acids can also interfere with the emulsification process when cooking the cheeses, which can result in a broken emulsion. To prevent this from occurring, acids are added to the cheese mixture after emulsification has already taken place.

Nutritional yeast flakes and other seasonings are often used in varied amounts to impart unique flavor or color characteristics, depending upon the variety of cheese.

A form will be needed for shaping and firming the block of cheese. Any glass, ceramic, metal or BPA-free plastic container that will hold a minimum of 2 cups liquid will work.

Consider the variety of cheese when choosing the shape of the container. For example, Brie is traditionally shaped in a round "wheel", whereas cheddar can be shaped in round, square or rectangular blocks, hence the title "Block and Wheel Cheeses".

Preparation and Cooking Technique

The Block and Wheel Cheeses are actually very easy to prepare; however, I've outlined the process in great detail so you will know what to expect. Familiarize yourself with the instructions and then follow them exactly as written to ensure success.

Before you begin, assemble all of your ingredients. In culinary terms this is known as *mise en place* (French for "putting in place"). Use exact, level measurements; please, no "eye-balling" measurements. Do not prepare the mixtures ahead of time; once mixed, they should be cooked immediately.

First, measure and set aside any fruit acids (vinegar or lemon juice) or lactic acid powder in a small dish and set aside near your cooking area. If the recipe calls for a combination of acids, mix them together in the small dish. Also prepare and set aside any special ingredients in a separate small dish as directed in the recipe, such as sautéed jalapeno, dried minced onion, red pepper flakes, etc.

Note: Although considered acidic, dry vermouth (used in Suisse), white wine (used in Provolone Affumicata) and tomato paste (used in Golden Cheddar, Americana and Gloucester with Onions and Chives), should not be set aside and should be included in the cheese mixture prior to cooking. This allows the alcohol in the vermouth or wine to evaporate during cooking and the golden color, created by the tomato paste, to fully develop.

Next, melt the coconut oil. To do this, remove the lid from the jar of coconut oil and place the jar in a microwave. Heat until the solid oil liquefies, about 30 seconds to 1 minute (this will depend upon the solidity of the coconut oil). Alternately, place the jar in about an inch of simmering water and melt the oil in the same manner. Repeated melting and re-hardening of the oil will not harm the oil as long as it's heated gently and high temperatures are not used.

While the coconut oil is melting, measure and pour the soymilk or almond milk into a 1-quart saucepan. Using a wire whisk (for stainless steel saucepans) or a silicone whisk (for non-stick saucepans), whisk in the tapioca flour and kappa carrageenan until smooth. Add any remaining seasoning ingredients and whisk vigorously until the ingredients are blended and the mixture is smooth.

Alternately, the ingredients can be mixed in a blender if you find this easier (this is actually more efficient when trying to incorporate thick ingredients such as miso and/or tomato paste). After blending, pour the mixture into the saucepan.

Measure the amount of coconut oil as directed in the formula and whisk this into the mixture. The coconut oil will not blend completely at this stage; this is normal. Place the saucepan over a medium-low gas flame. If using an electric stove, place over a medium-high setting. Set aside the whisk; it will no longer be needed.

Cooking the Cheese Mixture

Slowly and continually stir the mixture with a flexible spatula. The whisk is not recommended, as it is not as effective as the flexible spatula for scraping the sides of the saucepan as the mixture cooks. Stir in any special ingredients that have been set aside - but NOT the acids! As the mixture heats, it will begin to thicken and curdle (form lumps). If using an electric stove, immediately reduce the heat to medium-low as soon as the mixture thickens slightly and the curds begin to appear.

Begin stirring vigorously as the mixture continues to curdle and thicken. Scrape the sides of the saucepan with the spatula while stirring. After several minutes of cooking and stirring, the oil will begin to emulsify with the milk and other ingredients and transform into a smooth, glossy and gooey mass of melted cheese. If non-stick cookware is used, thicker cheese mixtures will pull away from the sides of the pan. When it has reached this stage, cooking is complete. If the mixture begins to bubble around the edges of the saucepan, cooking is definitely complete.

The consistency of the melted cheese will differ depending upon the variety of cheese; some cheese mixtures may be very thick, others may be more fluid. The entire cooking process should not take more than 5 to 6 minutes, sometimes less (and sometimes a few minutes more if using an electric stove). It is very important that the mixture be heated sufficiently to activate the carrageenan. If in doubt, use an instant read thermometer; the cheese is finished when the temperature reaches 175°F/79°C.

Important! If the oil begins to separate from the mixture while cooking, remove the saucepan immediately from the heat source and continue stirring vigorously until smooth. This can occur if the heat is too high and the mixture is being heated too quickly. Once recombined, finish the cheese according to the directions below.

If the mixture will not recombine (a broken emulsion), add a small splash of soymilk or almond milk (about 1 to 2 tablespoons), vigorously whip the mixture with the spatula until recombined and then finish the cheese according to the directions below. As a last resort, blitz the mixture with an immersion blender until recombined and then finish the cheese according to the directions below.

Finishing the Cheese

Remove the saucepan from the heat and immediately fold in any acids. Vigorously whip the mixture to ensure that the acids are blended thoroughly into the melted cheese.

Immediately transfer the melted cheese to the form using the spatula before it begins to set. Depending upon the variety of cheese, some mixtures will be thicker and others more fluid when pouring into the mold. Do not attempt to smooth the surface as the cheese will be very sticky; allow it to settle on its own. If the procedure was done correctly, the surface will begin to set almost immediately.

Let the cheese cool for 20 minutes and then cover with plastic wrap (omit covering Brie and Camembert). Refrigerate for a minimum of 6 hours to firm the cheese completely before being removing from the form.

After the cheese has been chilled and firmed completely, invert the form, covering the opening with your hand and sharply shake the form to loosen and remove the cheese. If the cheese does not loosen easily, run a table knife around the interior perimeter of the form to loosen the cheese. Blot the cheese with a paper towel to remove any moisture that has precipitated to the surface (except for Brie and Camembert).

A few cheeses require finishing procedures after firming. For example, the Brie and Camembert requires dusting with tapioca flour and a brief period of air-drying; Muenster requires rubbing the paprika into the surface of the cheese. Refer to the individual recipes for instructions.

Wrap the cheese snugly in additional paper towels (except for Brie and Camembert) and then wrap tightly in plastic wrap or seal in a zip-lock bag. Refrigerate for a minimum of 24 hours. The paper towel will absorb moisture released from the cheese during refrigeration and contribute to a firmer, drier texture.

Remove the paper towel and slice or shred as needed. Store the cheese in the refrigerator wrapped in a dry paper towel and then in plastic wrap or a zip-lock bag (squeeze out as much air as possible before sealing). Replace the paper towel every few days. The cheese will continue to firm as it ages and the moisture is absorbed by the paper towel. This method controls the drying process better, rather than exposing the cheese to air for an extended period, which can cause the exterior to dry out and crack (and possibly invite unwanted mold and bacterial contamination).

Please note that the Block and Wheel Cheeses have a higher melting point than dairy cheeses. Shredded cheese will melt easier than sliced cheese on grilled sandwiches. The cheeses will melt easily in moist heat conditions (such as in soups or casseroles) and they also melt easily in the microwave.

Troubleshooting Tips

Problem: The milk mixture is not reaching the curdling stage.

▶Possible cause and solution: Be patient. The mixture may take a few minutes to begin to thicken and curdle. Heating too quickly can result in a broken emulsion. If no thickening and curdling occurs after several minutes, the heat may be too low. Increase the heat slightly. If using an electric stove, begin heating the mixture over medium-high heat; when the mixture begins to curdle, immediately reduce the heat to medium-low.

Problem: The mixture appears oily as it transitions from the curdling stage to the smooth stage, or the oil has completely separated from the mixture while cooking.

▶Possible cause and solution: The heat is too high and the mixture is heating too quickly, causing the emulsion to break. Immediately remove the saucepan from the heat and stir vigorously until the mixture recombines. Once recombined, add any acids, stir vigorously and transfer to the mold. If the oil will not recombine, add 1 to 2 tablespoons of soymilk or almond milk and stir vigorously until recombined; or insert an immersion blender and process the mixture until recombined (please note that this will pulverize any special ingredients added to the cheese, so only use as a last resort).

Problem: The finished cheese will not firm properly or the cheese is softer than expected.

▶Possible cause and solution: The cheese was not cooked long enough. The mixture needs to reach the curdling stage and then transition to the smooth stage to create the proper texture. The cheese mixture needs to be heated properly to activate the carrageenan (175°F/79°C).

▶Possible cause and solution: The problem may be the quality of the carrageenan. Quality will vary from brand to brand. Kappa carrageenan produced by Molecule R™ is not compatible with the cheese formulas. Purchase carrageenan from a company with consistently high-quality kappa carrageenan, such as *ModernistPantry.com*

▶Possible cause and solution: The cheese was not sufficiently chilled. Be sure the cheese is sufficiently chilled before removing from the form.

▶Possible cause and solution: Some of the cheeses may be softer than what you remember of their dairy counterparts. The Block and Wheel Cheeses are not prepared with the same ingredients or in the same manner as dairy cheese. Be realistic and expect some differences in texture and flavor.

Problem: The finished cheese texture is soft and grainy.

▶Possible cause and solution: The emulsion broke while cooking the cheese. In the future, be sure the cooking heat is not too high. If the oil appears to be separating from the mixture while cooking, immediately remove the saucepan from the heat and stir vigorously until the mixture recombines. Once recombined, add any acids, stir vigorously and transfer to the mold. If the oil will not recombine, add 1 to 2 tablespoons of soymilk or almond milk and stir vigorously until recombined; or insert an immersion blender and process the mixture until recombined (please note that this will pulverize any special ingredients added to the cheese, so only use as a last resort).

Problem: The emulsion keeps breaking despite my best efforts and following directions.

▶Possible cause and solution: This is unusual. Something is wrong with either the ingredients you are using or the cooking temperature. DO NOT add the acids until the cheese mixture is cooked. If all else fails, cook the mixture while processing with an immersion blender. When the cheese mixture reaches 175°F/79°C (which can be determined using an instant read thermometer), it's ready to be transferred to the form.

Mozzarella Fior di Latte

Mozzarella Fior di Latte, which literally means "flower of milk", has a mild lactic flavor and a texture that is remarkably similar to low-moisture dairy mozzarella, which makes it excellent for fine shredding and melting. It's also an excellent cheese for preparing Saganaki (pg. 61), a pan-fried cheese dish. Mozzarella is traditionally a bland cheese which is used primarily for melting in recipes, rather than for snacking, so don't expect it to dazzle your tastebuds. For flavorful snacking variations, opt for Mozzarella di Tuscano (pg. 63) or Mozzarella di Campana (pg. 64).

For this recipe you will need a glass, ceramic, metal or BPA-free plastic container which will hold a minimum of 2 cups liquid; this will act as the form to shape the cheese.

Ingredients:

- ¾ tsp lactic acid powder or 1 T fresh lemon juice
- ⅔ cup organic **refined** coconut oil
- 1 and ⅓ cup pure soymilk or homemade Almond Milk (pg. 17)
- ¼ cup tapioca flour
- 4 tsp kappa carrageenan
- 1 and ¼ tsp fine sea salt or kosher salt

For Mozzarella Affumicata (smoked mozzarella), add 1 teaspoon liquid hickory smoke; or replace the salt with smoked sea salt.

Technique:

Before you begin, review the introduction to the Block and Wheel Cheeses on page 54. Gather all of your ingredients (*mise en place*).

Prepare the cheese according to the Preparation and Cooking Technique instructions on page 57.

Saganaki

Saganaki refers to various Greek dishes prepared in a small frying pan called a *saganaki*, the best-known being an appetizer of fried cheese. Traditionally, dairy Kasseri cheese is used, but Mozzarella Fior di Latte or Muenster works well for this non-dairy version.

To prepare Saganaki, the cheese is lightly dredged in flour and then fried in a skillet until it is golden and crisp on the outside and melted on the inside. Optionally after frying, the skillet can be doused with brandy or cognac and the cheese flambéed tableside, traditionally with a shout of *Opa!* The bubbly, melted cheese is seasoned with a squeeze of fresh lemon juice and a generous sprinkle of black pepper and then eaten with bread or crackers.

Saganaki ingredients:

- Mozzarella Fior di Latte (pg. 60) or Muenster (pg. 74)
- unbleached all-purpose flour or rice flour
- olive oil
- optional: 2 T brandy or cognac (or less if not using the whole block of cheese)
- ½ large lemon, seeds removed
- coarse ground black pepper, to taste
- crusty bread or crackers

Technique:

Slice the cheese into slabs, no more than ¼-inch thick. Dredge the slices in flour and set aside.

Lightly oil a non-stick skillet with the olive oil and place over medium-high heat. When the skillet is hot, fry the cheese until the slices look visibly melted halfway through. With a lightly oiled flexible spatula, carefully flip the slices over. Flip gently as to not dislodge the crispy exterior from the melted cheese. Continue to cook another minute or two.

Immediately transfer the skillet tableside and place on a trivet. Season the cheese with a squeeze of lemon juice and black pepper to taste. Serve with crusty bread or crackers.

Optional flambé (do not use this technique unless you enjoy the flavor of brandy or cognac): After transferring the skillet tableside, douse the skillet with the brandy or cognac and ignite with a long match. Let the cheese flame until it extinguishes on its own. Season the cheese with a squeeze of lemon juice and black pepper to taste. Serve with crusty bread or crackers. *Opa!*

Eggplant Rollatini

Tender sliced eggplant is rolled around a seasoned ricotta and parmesan filling, topped with marinara sauce and mozzarella and then baked to perfection.

Ingredients:

- 2 large eggplants, peeled and ends removed
- olive oil
- 2 cups Creamy Ricotta (pg. 91)
- 3 T grated Hard Parmesan (pg. 97) or Grated Parmesan (pg. 99)
- ¼ cup fresh, finely chopped basil or 1 T dried basil
- sea salt or kosher salt and black pepper to taste
- 6 oz shredded Mozzarella Fior di Latte (pg. 60), about 1 and ½ cup
- 2 cups prepared Chef's Best Marinara Sauce (pg. 93), or similar

Technique:

Preheat oven to 450°F.

Peel and slice the eggplant lengthwise, about ¼ to ½-inch thick. Oil a baking sheet (or two sheets if available to accommodate all the eggplant slices) and lay the slices in a single layer. Brush lightly with olive oil and sprinkle with salt. Bake about 10 to 12 minutes or until the eggplant is softened. This ensures easy rolling. Transfer to a plate to cool.

Reduce oven heat to 400°F.

In a bowl, combine the ricotta, 3 tablespoons parmesan, ½ cup shredded mozzarella, basil and salt and pepper to taste.

In a shallow casserole dish, spread about ½ cup marinara sauce evenly on the bottom. Set aside.

On a work surface, spread about 2 tablespoons of the ricotta mixture on an eggplant slice. Roll up and place into the casserole dish, seam side down. Repeat with each slice.

Top the rollatini with the remaining mozzarella and then with the remaining sauce. Bake uncovered for about 30 minutes or until the cheese is nicely melted.

Mozzarella di Tuscano

Mozzarella di Tuscano is a variation of Mozzarella Fior di Latte flavored with sun-dried tomatoes, dried sweet basil, sautéed garlic and a hint of red pepper. It's a superb cold snacking cheese but melts beautifully too.

Mozzarella ingredients:

- ⅔ cup organic **refined** coconut oil
- ¾ tsp lactic acid powder or 1 T fresh lemon juice
- 1 and ⅓ cup pure soymilk or homemade Almond Milk (pg. 17)
- ¼ cup tapioca flour
- 4 tsp kappa carrageenan
- 1 and ¼ tsp fine sea salt or kosher salt

Special seasoning ingredients:

- 1 tsp olive oil
- 3 cloves garlic, minced
- ¼ cup finely diced sun-dried tomatoes
- 1 tsp dried sweet basil
- ½ teaspoon red pepper flakes

Technique:

Before you begin, review the introduction to the Block and Wheel Cheeses on page 54. Gather all of your ingredients (*mise en place*).

In a small skillet, prepare the special seasoning ingredients by briefly sautéing the garlic in the olive oil over medium-low heat. Do not let the garlic burn. Transfer to a small dish; mix in the sun-dried tomatoes, basil and red pepper flakes. Set aside.

Prepare the cheese according to the Preparation and Cooking Technique instructions on page 57. Stir in the garlic/tomato/herb mixture while cooking the cheese.

Mozzarella di Campana

Mozzarella di Campana is a variation of Mozzarella Fior di Latte flavored with dried oregano, dried sweet basil, minced fresh garlic, coarse ground black pepper and a hint of red pepper. It's a superb cold snacking cheese but melts beautifully too.

Mozzarella ingredients:

- ⅔ cup organic **refined** coconut oil
- ¾ tsp lactic acid powder or 1 T fresh lemon juice
- 1 and ⅓ cup pure soymilk or homemade Almond Milk (pg. 17)
- ¼ cup tapioca flour
- 4 tsp kappa carrageenan
- 1 and ¼ tsp fine sea salt or kosher salt

Special seasoning ingredients:

- 2 cloves garlic, minced
- 1 tsp dried oregano
- 1 tsp dried sweet basil
- ½ tsp coarse ground black pepper
- ½ tsp red pepper flakes

Technique:

Before you begin, review the introduction to the Block and Wheel Cheeses on page 54. Gather all of your ingredients (*mise en place*).

Mix together the special seasoning ingredients in a small dish and set aside near your cooking area. Prepare the cheese according to the Preparation and Cooking Technique instructions on page 57. Stir in the special seasoning ingredients while cooking the cheese.

Mozzarella Fresco

Mozzarella Fresco is a semi-soft cheese with a mild lactic flavor. It's cooked in the same manner as Mozzarella Fior di Latte, but rather than being shaped in a block form, it's scooped into round balls and chilled in a brine solution. Mozzarella Fresco is a component of Insalata Mozzarella Fresco (pg. 66), a variation of the popular Caprese salad. It also melts nicely when sliced and baked on bruschetta or pizza.

Brine ingredients:

- 4 cups water
- 2 tsp sea salt or kosher salt

Mozzarella ingredients:

- ¾ tsp lactic acid powder or 1 T fresh lemon juice
- ⅔ cup organic refined coconut oil
- 1 and ⅓ cup plain pure soymilk or homemade Almond Milk (pg. 17)
- ¼ cup tapioca flour
- 1 T kappa carrageenan
- 1 and ¼ tsp sea salt or kosher salt

Technique:

First, combine the brine ingredients and chill until very cold.

Before you begin, review the introduction to the Block and Wheel Cheeses on page 54. Gather all of your ingredients (*mise en place*) and set the chilled brine near your work area.

Prepare the cheese according to the Preparation and Cooking Technique instructions on page 57. After cooking, remove the saucepan from the heat and place on a trivet or other heatproof surface near your work area.

With an ice cream scoop or ladle, scoop up the hot cheese mixture, and with a spoon in your opposite hand, scrape off any cheese that is hanging from the sides of the scoop back into the saucepan. This will help create more uniformly round balls of cheese. Add the scoop of cheese to the chilled brine. The exterior of the cheese ball will firm upon contact. Repeat with the remaining cheese mixture.

Refrigerate for several hours until the brine is re-chilled and the mozzarella balls have firmed (keep in mind that the cheese will still be soft).

Drain with a slotted spoon and set on a paper towel to blot excess water before using in recipes. Stored in the brine, the mozzarella should keep for about 1 week in the refrigerator. Freezing is not recommended for this cheese.

Insalata Mozzarella Fresco

This is my own variation of the popular Caprese salad. Stewed tomatoes are combined with sliced sweet onions, fresh basil, fresh mozzarella and balsamic vinaigrette and then garnished with caperberries for a cool and refreshing salad. This is one of my favorites and I think you'll enjoy it too.

This salad needs to be prepared at least a day ahead to allow time for the salad ingredients to marinate, so plan accordingly. Also try serving this salad over toasted crusty bread rounds or croutons; the crisp bread soaks up the flavorful juice and is absolutely delicious!

Ingredients:

- 2 cans (14 oz. each) stewed tomatoes with the juice
  or 3 cups home-stewed or home canned tomatoes with juice
- 1 small, sweet yellow onion, thinly sliced
- 1 bunch fresh basil, chiffonade (sliced into ribbons)
- ⅔ cup balsamic vinaigrette
- Mozzarella Fresco (pg. 65), ¼-inch thick slices
- sea salt or kosher salt and coarse ground black pepper, to taste
- optional garnish: caperberries*

*Caperberries are the fruit of the Mediterranean caper bush, whereas capers are the small flower buds.

Technique:

Prepare the fresh mozzarella and refrigerate. In a large bowl or food storage container with a lid, combine all of the ingredients except the mozzarella. Cover and refrigerate overnight. To serve, spoon the salad into a serving bowl and top with slices of the mozzarella. Garnish with the optional caperberries and additional fresh basil if desired.

Pizza Margherita

Pizza Margherita is a classic pizza prepared according to a recipe of the Italian chef Raffaelle Esposito and is named after Queen Margherita of Savoy. The tomatoes, mozzarella cheese and basil represent the colors of the Italian flag. This recipe yields one large pizza.

Ingredients for the pizza dough:

- 2 tsp organic sugar
- 1 cup warm water
- 1 package (¼ oz.) active dry yeast
- 1 T sea salt or kosher salt
- olive oil
- 3 cups bread flour or all-purpose flour, plus more for dusting

Ingredients for the topping:

- 1 cup crushed tomatoes
- 1 tsp organic sugar
- 2 T olive oil
- sea salt or kosher salt and coarse ground black pepper, to taste
- ½ cup fresh basil leaves, coarsely chopped or julienned
- ½ cup shaved Hard Parmesan (pg. 97) or Grated Parmesan (pg. 99)
- ½ pound Mozzarella Fresco (pg. 65), sliced ¼-inch thick

Technique:

To prepare the pizza dough, dissolve the sugar in the warm water in a small bowl. Proof the yeast by adding to the sugar/water mixture; stir gently to dissolve. Leave the mixture undisturbed until the yeast begins to foam, about 10 minutes. If the yeast does not produce foam, it is inactive; purchase new yeast with an extended expiration date.

Add the yeast mixture to a large mixing bowl and stir in the salt and 2 tablespoons of olive oil. With a sturdy spoon or spatula, stir in the flour a little at a time until all the flour has been incorporated. Mix until the dough starts to hold together and transfer to a floured work surface. Begin to knead the dough using the heel of your hand. Get a feel for the dough by squeezing a small amount together: if it's crumbly, add more water; if it's sticky, add more flour - 1 tablespoon at a time. Knead until the dough is smooth and elastic, about 3 minutes.

Form the dough into a round ball, place in a lightly oiled bowl and turn it over to coat with the oil. Cover with plastic wrap or a damp towel and let it rise in a warm spot until doubled in size, about 1 hour.

While the dough is rising, prepare the sauce. In a food processor, combine the tomatoes, sugar and olive oil and process until smooth, season with salt and black pepper to taste. Set aside.

Preheat oven to 475° F and, if you have one, place a pizza stone on the bottom rack of the oven.

Turn the dough onto a lightly floured work surface. Roll and stretch the dough with your hands into a cylinder. Divide the dough into 2 equal pieces (the dough recipe will yield enough for 2 pizzas; reserve the second portion for another pizza or other recipes such as calzones, strombolis, etc.) Cover and let the pizza portion of dough rest for 10 minutes to relax the gluten before rolling out.

Lightly dust a large cutting board and your rolling pin with flour. With the rolling pin, roll out the piece of dough into a large circle, about ⅛-inch thick. Spread the sauce evenly over the dough leaving a ½-inch border along the edges. Sprinkle the basil on top of the sauce and then top with the mozzarella slices and parmesan. If you don't have a pizza stone, slide the pizza onto a large baking sheet and place in the hot oven. Otherwise, slide the pizza directly onto the pizza stone in the oven. Bake about 8 minutes, or until the cheese is melted and the edges are golden brown and crisp.

Remove from the oven and garnish with fresh basil leaves if desired.

Provolone Affumicata
(Smoked Provolone)

Provolone Affumicata is a firm Italian cheese with a smoky flavor that adds panache to cold sandwiches or when melted on burgers or grilled sandwiches. The firm texture of this cheese makes it easy to slice very thin, especially when using an electric deli slicer.

For this recipe you will need a glass, ceramic, metal or BPA-free plastic container which will hold a minimum of 2 cups liquid; this will act as the form to shape the cheese.

Ingredients:

- ½ cup organic **refined** coconut oil
- 1 and ⅓ cup pure soymilk or homemade Almond Milk (pg. 17)
- ¼ cup tapioca flour
- 2 T mellow white miso paste
- 1 T dry white wine*
- 4 tsp kappa carrageenan
- 2 tsp liquid hickory smoke
- ½ tsp fine sea salt or kosher salt
- ¼ tsp onion powder

*The wine can be omitted for health or ethical reasons but this will alter the flavor slightly.

Technique:

Before you begin, review the introduction to the Block and Wheel Cheeses on page 54. Gather all of your ingredients (*mise en place*).

Prepare the cheese according to the Preparation and Cooking Technique instructions on page 57.

French Brie and Camembert

Brie is named after the French region from which it originated. It is a soft, spreadable table cheese with a rich, creamy and buttery flavor. Camembert is very similar to Brie, but has deeper, earthy undertones.

Tapioca flour is used to mimic the exterior white mold bloom in both cheeses and white truffle oil is used in the Camembert to produce its characteristic earthy flavor. Both cheeses are excellent when served at room temperature with fresh fruit and crackers or they can be baked "en croûte" (wrapped in flaky puff pastry with optional toppings and baked until melted).

For this recipe you will need a round glass, ceramic, metal or BPA-free plastic container which will hold a minimum of 2 cups liquid; this will act as the form to shape the wheel of cheese. Line the form with plastic wrap with excess hanging over the edge. This will help lift the cheese from the form after firming.

Cheese ingredients:

- 2 tsp raw apple cider vinegar
- ½ cup organic **refined** coconut oil
- 1 and ⅓ cup pure soymilk or homemade Almond Milk (pg. 17)
- ¼ cup tapioca flour
- 1 T nutritional yeast flakes
- 1 T mellow white miso paste
- 1 and ¼ tsp kappa carrageenan
- 1 tsp fine sea salt or kosher salt
- ½ tsp to 1 tsp white truffle oil, to taste (for Camembert only)

Set aside an additional 2 T tapioca flour for the mold bloom.

Technique:

Before you begin, review the introduction to the Block and Wheel Cheeses on page 54. Gather all of your ingredients (*mise en place*). Prepare the cheese according to the Preparation and Cooking Technique instructions on page 57.

After cooking and transferring to the form, let the cheese cool for 20 minutes and then refrigerate uncovered for a minimum of 8 hours. This will allow the surface of the cheese to dry slightly while firming in the refrigerator.

To remove the cheese from the container after firming, place a plate over the top of the form and invert, shaking gently. Peel away the plastic wrap and discard. Handle the cheese carefully as it will be soft and rather sticky. For preparing Brie or Camembert en Croûte, proceed to the recipe on the following page.

Otherwise, generously dust the cheese on all sides with tapioca flour. This will help dry the exterior, reduce stickiness and imitate the "mold bloom". Set the cheese on a parchment-lined plate or baker's cooling rack with the driest side on the bottom (the side that was exposed to air while refrigerating). Place the cheese in the refrigerator to air-dry for an additional 8 hours. This will help create a soft "rind".

Let the cheese come to room temperature before serving. Store the cheese in the refrigerator in a zip-lock bag or securely wrapped in plastic.

Brie or Camembert en Croûte
with Caramelized Mushrooms, Onions and Walnuts

Rich and buttery Brie (or earthy Camembert) is baked in a puff pastry crust with caramelized mushrooms, onions and walnuts. This elegant appetizer is sure to impress. If desired, the filling can be replaced with fruit preserves, such as fig or apricot and any lightly toasted nuts that suit your fancy.

Ingredients:

- 1 round of Brie or Camembert cheese (see the recipe on the previous page)
- 1 sheet dairy and egg-free frozen puff pastry dough (e.g., Pepperidge Farm™)
- 1 T Better Butter (pg. 28) or Vital Butter (pg. 33)
- 4 large white or cremini mushrooms (about 4 oz)
- ½ medium onion, sliced thin and then chopped
- ¼ cup chopped walnuts (optional)
- ¼ tsp dried thyme
- a few pinches of salt and coarse ground black pepper
- a splash of dry white wine (e.g., Chardonnay, Sauvignon Blanc)

Technique:

Prepare the Brie or Camembert according to the directions. Let the cheese come to room temperature while the puff pastry dough thaws for about 30 to 40 minutes. Preheat the oven to 400°F.

In a skillet over medium heat, sauté the onions, mushrooms and walnuts in the butter until the onions are translucent. Add the thyme, a sprinkle of salt and pepper and the splash of optional wine and continue to sauté until the liquid has evaporated and the mushrooms and onions are browned nicely. Set aside to cool.

Lay out the puff pastry dough on a lightly oiled or parchment-lined baking sheet and center the cheese in the middle. Top with the mushroom/onion/walnut mixture. Try to keep the mixture mounded on top of the cheese but if some falls to the sides, don't worry about it. Begin to fold the edges of the pastry dough over the mixture and cheese.

Bake until golden brown on top, about 30 to 35 minutes. Slice and serve immediately.

For a caramelized onion and fig preserve filling, caramelize only the onion in butter as described above. Transfer to a small dish to cool. Stir in a few tablespoons of fig preserves and proceed with the recipe as usual.

Pepper Jack

Pepper Jack has a firm texture and piquant flavor that is wonderful for snacking with crackers. It can also be sliced and served on cold sandwiches, melted on grilled sandwiches or shredded and used in recipes. For a mild Monterey Jack, simply omit the green chili and red pepper.

For this recipe you will need a glass, ceramic, metal or BPA-free plastic container which will hold a minimum of 2 cups liquid; this will act as the form to shape the cheese.

Ingredients:

- 1 large jalapeno or serrano chili
- 1 tsp red pepper flakes
- 2 tsp raw apple cider vinegar
- ¼ tsp lactic acid powder or 1 tsp fresh lemon juice
- ⅔ cup organic **refined** coconut oil
- 1 and ⅓ cup pure soymilk or homemade Almond Milk (pg. 17)
- ¼ cup tapioca flour
- 2 T nutritional yeast flakes
- 4 tsp kappa carrageenan
- 1 and ¼ tsp fine sea salt or kosher salt

Technique:

Before you begin, review the introduction to the Block and Wheel Cheeses on page 54. Gather all of your ingredients (*mise en place*).

Seed and very finely mince the jalapeno or serrano chili. Wear gloves if you have sensitive skin or be sure to wash your hands thoroughly after handling. Spray a small skillet with a little cooking oil spray and sauté the minced pepper over medium-low heat until tender; be careful not to burn the pepper. Transfer to a small dish, mix in the red pepper flakes and set aside near your cooking area.

Prepare the cheese according to the Preparation and Cooking Technique instructions on page 57. Stir in the pepper mixture while cooking the cheese.

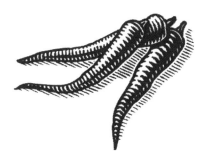

Dill Havarti

Dill Havarti is a creamy, buttery, slightly acidic, semi-soft table cheese. The dill adds a wonderful fresh herb flavor without being overpowering. It's ideal for slicing and serving on crackers or cold sandwiches and superb for melting on grilled sandwiches.

For this recipe you will need a glass, ceramic, metal or BPA-free plastic container which will hold a minimum of 2 cups liquid; this will act as the form to shape the cheese.

Ingredients:

- ½ tsp lactic acid powder or 2 tsp fresh lemon juice
- 2 tsp raw apple cider vinegar
- ⅔ cup organic **refined** coconut oil
- 1 and ⅓ cup pure soymilk or homemade Almond Milk (pg. 17)
- ¼ cup tapioca flour
- 4 tsp nutritional yeast flakes
- 1 T kappa carrageenan
- 1 and ¼ tsp fine sea salt or kosher salt
- 2 T finely minced fresh dill

Technique:

Before you begin, review the introduction to the Block and Wheel Cheeses on page 54. Gather all of your ingredients (*mise en place*).

Prepare the cheese according to the Preparation and Cooking Technique instructions on page 57. Stir in the dill (or other variations) while cooking the cheese.

Variations:

- ❖ For Caraway Havarti, replace the dill with 1 teaspoon caraway seeds lightly crushed with a mortar and pestle.
- ❖ For Garlic Pepper Havarti, replace the dill with 1 tablespoon cracked black pepper and 2 cloves finely minced garlic.
- ❖ For Onion Pepper Dill Havarti, add 1 T dried minced onion and 2 tsp cracked black pepper to the dill havarti mixture.

Suisse

Suisse is a firm cheese with a mild, nutty and distinctive Swiss cheese flavor. It can be thinly sliced and served on cold sandwiches, grilled and melted on hot sandwiches or shredded and used in recipes. The characteristic Swiss cheese appearance is created by punching holes in the finished cheese with an apple corer; however, this is purely optional.

For this recipe you will need a glass, ceramic, metal or BPA-free plastic container which will hold a minimum of 2 cups liquid; this will act as the form to shape the cheese.

Ingredients:

- ½ cup organic **refined** coconut oil
- 1 and ⅓ cup pure soymilk or homemade Almond Milk (pg. 17)
- ¼ cup tapioca flour
- 2 T nutritional yeast flakes
- 2 T mellow white miso paste
- 2 T extra-dry vermouth*
- 4 tsp kappa carrageenan
- ½ tsp fine sea salt or kosher salt
- ½ tsp dry ground mustard
- ¼ tsp ground coriander

*The vermouth can be omitted for health or ethical reasons, but this will alter the flavor profile significantly.

Technique:

Before you begin, review the introduction to the Block and Wheel Cheeses on page 54. Gather all of your ingredients (*mise en place*).

Prepare the cheese according to the Preparation and Cooking Technique instructions on page 57.

Muenster

Muenster is a cheese from the United States, not to be confused with the French variety, Munster. Non-dairy Muenster has a semi-soft texture with an orange "rind" and a mild, buttery flavor. The coloration of the "rind" is created by rubbing the exterior of the cheese with sweet paprika. Slices are ideal for cold sandwiches and for melting on burgers or other grilled sandwiches. It's also an excellent cheese for preparing Saganaki, a pan-fried cheese dish (pg. 61).

For this recipe you will need a glass, ceramic, metal or BPA-free plastic container which will hold a minimum of 2 cups liquid; this will act as the form to shape the cheese.

Ingredients:

- 1 tsp sweet paprika (to color the exterior)
- 2 tsp raw apple cider vinegar
- ⅔ cup organic **refined** coconut oil
- 1 and ⅓ cup pure soymilk or homemade Almond Milk (pg. 17)
- ¼ cup tapioca flour
- 2 T nutritional yeast flakes
- 1 T kappa carrageenan
- 1 and ¼ tsp fine sea salt or kosher salt
- ¼ tsp dry ground mustard
- ⅛ tsp onion powder

Technique:

Before you begin, review the introduction to the Block and Wheel Cheeses on page 54. Gather all of your ingredients (*mise en place*).

Lightly mist the interior of the cheese form with cooking oil. Add the paprika and turn the form side to side and back and forth to dust the interior with the spice. It's not essential to coat it evenly, just do the best you can. Discard any excess and loose spice by inverting and tapping the container. Set aside.

Prepare the cheese according to the Preparation and Cooking Technique instructions on page 57.

After the cheese has been chilled and firmed completely, invert the form, covering the opening with your hand and sharply shake the form to loosen and remove the cheese. If the cheese does not loosen easily, run a table knife around the interior perimeter of the form to loosen the cheese. Gently rub the cheese to distribute the paprika evenly.

Wrap the cheese snugly in a paper towel and then wrap tightly in plastic wrap or seal in a zip-lock bag. Refrigerate for 24 hours. The paper towel will absorb any moisture released from the cheese during refrigeration and contribute to a firmer, drier texture.

Remove the paper towel and slice or shred as needed. Store the cheese in the refrigerator wrapped in a dry paper towel and then plastic wrap or a zip-lock bag (squeeze out as much air as possible before sealing). Replace the paper towel every few days.

Smoked Gouda

Gouda is an iconic Dutch cheese. My dairy-free version produces a firm table cheese with a distinctive smoke flavor which is very reminiscent of dairy smoked Gouda. It's wonderful for snacking with crackers but adds a gourmet touch when sliced for cold sandwiches or melted on grilled sandwiches.

For this recipe you will need a glass, ceramic, metal or BPA-free plastic container which will hold a minimum of 2 cups liquid; this will act as the form to shape the cheese.

Ingredients:

- ⅔ cup organic **refined** coconut oil
- 1 and ⅓ cup pure soymilk or homemade Almond Milk (pg. 17)
- ¼ cup tapioca flour
- 2 T nutritional yeast flakes
- 4 tsp kappa carrageenan
- 2 tsp liquid hickory smoke
- 1 and ¼ tsp fine sea salt or kosher salt
- 1 tsp vegan Worcestershire sauce
- ½ tsp onion powder

Technique:

Before you begin, review the introduction to the Block and Wheel Cheeses on page 54. Gather all of your ingredients (*mise en place*).

Prepare the cheese according to the Preparation and Cooking Technique instructions on page 57.

Smoked Gouda, Spinach and Artichoke Dip

Smoked Gouda and Hard Parmesan cheeses are blended with a creamy purée of spinach, artichokes, onions and garlic and baked to perfection.

Ingredients:

- 2 T olive oil
- 1 small onion, chopped
- 2 cloves garlic, minced
- 1 pkg (10 oz) frozen spinach
- 1 can (14 oz) artichoke hearts, rinsed and drained well
- 6 oz shredded Smoked Gouda (pg. 75), about 1 and ½ cup
- ½ cup Cultured Sour Cream (pg. 37)
- ¼ cup No-Eggy Mayo (pg. 140)
- 2 T grated Hard Parmesan (pg. 97)
- fine sea salt or kosher salt and coarse ground black pepper, to taste

Technique:

Thaw and press the spinach to remove as much liquid as possible (a tofu press is ideal for this).

Preheat the oven to 350°F and lightly oil a shallow baking dish.

In a skillet over medium heat, sauté the onion in the vegetable oil until the onion is translucent. Add the garlic and spinach. Sauté until the onion begins to lightly brown. This will take several minutes. Transfer to a food processor. Add the artichoke hearts to the food processor with the spinach/onion/garlic mixture. Pulse a few times to coarsely chop but do not purée.

Transfer to a mixing bowl; add the cheese, sour cream, mayonnaise and parmesan and stir thoroughly to combine. Season the mixture with salt and pepper to taste. Transfer to the baking dish and bake uncovered for 30 minutes.

Set the oven on "broil" and broil for an additional 1 to 2 minutes or until lightly brown on top. Serve hot with crackers, bread or crudités. To keep warm for special occasions, transfer to a chafing dish and heat over a low flame.

To serve in a bread bowl, tear chunks from the interior of a round loaf of crusty bread to hollow out the loaf. Reserve the bread chunks for dipping. Wrap the bread bowl in foil and heat in a warm oven. Transfer the cheese mixture to the warm bread bowl and serve immediately; otherwise keep warm in the oven until ready to serve.

Golden Cheddar

Admittedly, replicating the flavor of dairy cheddar cheese has been my most difficult challenge, especially in an uncultured, "instant" cheese. Golden Cheddar is a firm cheese with a flavor reminiscent of mild dairy cheddar cheese. Thin slices are ideal for cold sandwiches or for melting on burgers or other grilled sandwiches. Golden Cheddar can also be shredded and used in your favorite recipes. Try the Smoky Cheddar and Smoky Chipotle Cheddar variations too.

For this recipe you will need a glass, ceramic, metal or BPA-free plastic container which will hold a minimum of 2 cups liquid; this will act as the form to shape the cheese.

Ingredients:

- 2 tsp raw apple cider vinegar
- ½ cup organic **refined** coconut oil
- 1 and ⅓ cup pure soymilk or homemade Almond Milk (pg. 17)
- ¼ cup tapioca flour
- ¼ cup nutritional yeast flakes
- 4 tsp kappa carrageenan
- 1 T mellow white miso paste
- 1 T tomato paste or 1 and ½ tsp tomato powder
- 1 tsp fine sea salt or kosher salt
- ½ tsp dry ground mustard
- ½ tsp onion powder

Variations:

- ❖ For Smoky Cheddar, omit the vinegar and add 2 tsp liquid hickory smoke.
- ❖ For Smoky Chipotle Cheddar, omit the vinegar and add 2 tsp liquid mesquite smoke; replace the tomato paste or powder with 1 teaspoon chipotle chili powder.

Technique:

Before you begin, review the introduction to the Block and Wheel Cheeses on page 54. Gather all of your ingredients (*mise en place*).

Prepare the cheese according to the Preparation and Cooking Technique instructions on page 57.

Note: Golden Cheddar is a firm cheese; however, it's not a hard cheese like dairy cheddar, so don't expect an exact replica. The cheese will benefit from refrigeration for several days wrapped in paper towels to absorb the excess moisture (be sure to change the towels daily). The cheese also has a tendency to clump when shredded. Dairy cheddars also have a tendency to clump when shredded and this is why commercial packaging of shredded dairy cheddar often includes powdered cellulose to discourage clumping.

Broccoli Cheddar Soup

Tender bits of broccoli and shredded carrot are bathed in a rich, creamy and cheesy cheddar soup base. This recipe yields 4 to 6 servings.

Ingredients:

- 4 cups Golden Stock (pg. 79) or commercial vegan "chicken" broth
- ¼ cup olive oil
- 1 medium onion, peeled and diced
- 1 carrot, peeled and shredded
- ⅓ cup unbleached all-purpose flour or rice flour
- 12 oz. broccoli florets, coarsely chopped (about 4 cups by volume)
- ¼ tsp ground nutmeg
- 1 cup plain unsweetened non-dairy milk
- 6 oz. Golden Cheddar (pg. 77), shredded (about 1 and ½ cup)
- sea salt or kosher salt and coarse ground black pepper, to taste

Technique:

Prepare and strain the stock; this can be done in advance or just prior to making the soup.

Add the olive oil to a large cooking pot and place over medium heat. Sauté the onions and carrots until tender, about 5 minutes. Avoid browning the vegetables.

Sprinkle in the flour, stir until blended and cook until the flour emits a nutty aroma, about 1 minute.

Add the stock in increments while stirring. Add the chopped broccoli and nutmeg and bring to a brief boil. The stock should just barely cover the broccoli. Resist adding more stock. Reduce the heat to a gentle simmer, partially cover the pot and cook, stirring frequently, for about 20 minutes or until the broccoli is tender. Avoid overcooking or the broccoli will become mushy and disintegrate completely.

Add the milk and shredded cheese and stir until the cheese is melted and the soup is heated through; season with salt and pepper to taste.

Golden Stock

This basic stock has a golden color and a light herbal flavor. It can be used as a base for preparing sauces, golden gravies and a variety of soups and stews, such as Broccoli Cheddar Soup (pg. 78) and Potato Cheese Soup (pg. 81). This recipe yields 8 cups of prepared stock.

Ingredients:

- 8 cups (2 quarts) water
- outer layers from 1 large onion
- peelings from 1 large carrot or 1 T dehydrated carrot flakes
- 6 parsley stems
- 1 clove garlic, crushed
- 2 T plus 2 tsp nutritional yeast flakes
- 2 tsp fine sea salt or kosher salt
- 1 tsp organic sugar
- ½ tsp poultry seasoning

Technique:

Remove the paper skin from the onion and discard. Add the tough, outer layers of the onion to a large cooking pot with the water. Add the carrot peelings (or dehydrated flakes) and additional ingredients. Reserve the peeled carrot and the tender portion of the onion for broth, soups, stews or other recipes.

Bring the stock to a boil. Reduce the heat to low, cover the cooking pot and cook for 30 minutes. Using a slotted spoon, remove the large solids. If using the stock immediately, add vegetables, herbs and spices as desired or as specified in a recipe to create a fully seasoned broth; season with additional salt to taste. For most recipe applications, the stock does not require clarification to remove the nutritional yeast and seasoning sediment.

If a clear stock is desired, let the liquid cool to room temperature and then pour into a sealable container, discarding any sediment that has settled on the bottom of the cooking pot. Refrigerate for up to 10 days. Any micro-fine particles will settle, further clarifying the stock. Decant the clear portion for use in recipes as needed. The stock can also be stored in the freezer for up to 1 month.

Americana

Americana is a firm cheese with a mild American cheese flavor. Thin slices are superb for cold sandwiches or for melting on burgers or other grilled sandwiches. Americana can also be gently shredded and used in your favorite recipes.

For this recipe you will need a glass, ceramic, metal or BPA-free plastic container which will hold a minimum of 2 cups liquid; this will act as the form to shape the cheese.

Ingredients:

- ¼ tsp lactic acid powder or 1 tsp fresh lemon juice
- ½ cup organic **refined** coconut oil
- 1 and ⅓ cup pure soymilk or homemade Almond Milk (pg. 17)
- ¼ cup tapioca flour
- 3 T nutritional yeast flakes
- 1 T mellow white miso paste
- 4 tsp kappa carrageenan
- 2 tsp tomato paste or 1 tsp tomato powder
- 1 tsp fine sea salt or kosher salt
- ½ tsp dry ground mustard
- ½ tsp onion powder

Technique:

Before you begin, review the introduction to the Block and Wheel Cheeses on page 54. Gather all of your ingredients (*mise en place*).

Prepare the cheese according to the Preparation and Cooking Technique instructions on page 57.

Potato Cheese Soup

Tender chunks of potato and celery are bathed in a rich, creamy and cheesy soup base. This recipe yields about 6 servings.

Ingredients:

- 4 cups Golden Stock (pg. 79) or commercial vegan "chicken" broth
- 1 and ½ lbs russet potatoes (about 3 average size russets)
- ¼ cup olive oil
- 1 medium onion, peeled and diced
- 2 large ribs of celery, chopped into ½-inch pieces
- ⅓ cup unbleached all-purpose flour or rice flour
- 2 sprigs fresh thyme leaves or ½ dried thyme leaves
- 1 bay leaf
- 1 cup plain unsweetened non-dairy milk
- 6 oz. Americana (pg. 80), shredded (about 1 and ½ cup)
- sea salt or kosher salt and coarse ground black pepper, to taste
- optional garnish: cooked and crumbled vegan bacon

Technique:

Prepare and strain the stock; this can be done in advance or just prior to making the soup. Peel and dice the potatoes and then place them in a cool water bath to prevent oxidation (turning brown).

Add the olive oil to a large cooking pot and place over medium heat. Sauté the onions and celery about 5 minutes or until barely tender; avoid browning the vegetables. Sprinkle in the flour, stir until blended and cook until the flour emits a nutty aroma, about 1 minute. Incorporate the stock in increments while stirring. Drain the potatoes thoroughly in a colander and then add to the cooking pot.

Add the thyme and bay leaf and bring the soup to a brief boil. Reduce the heat to a gentle simmer, partially cover the pot and cook for about 45 minutes or until the potatoes are very tender and to the point of disintegrating, stirring occasionally.

Add the milk and shredded cheese and stir until the cheese is melted and the soup is heated through; season with salt and pepper to taste. Remove the bay leaf and ladle the soup into individual serving bowls. Garnish with optional cooked and crumbled vegan bacon.

Gloucester with Onions and Chives

Gloucester is a firm, golden cheddar-style cheese with a savory onion and chive flavor. Slice and serve with your favorite crackers. Thin slices add a gourmet touch to cold sandwiches or when melted on burgers or other grilled sandwiches.

For this recipe you will need a glass, ceramic, metal or BPA-free plastic container which will hold a minimum of 2 cups liquid; this will act as the form to shape the cheese.

Ingredients:

- 1 T dried minced onion
- 1 T freeze-dried chives
- 2 tsp raw apple cider vinegar
- ½ cup organic **refined** coconut oil
- 1 and ⅓ cup pure soymilk or homemade Almond Milk (pg. 17)
- ¼ cup tapioca flour
- ¼ cup nutritional yeast flakes
- 4 tsp kappa carrageenan
- 2 tsp tomato paste or 1 tsp tomato powder
- 1 tsp fine sea salt or kosher salt
- ½ tsp dry ground mustard

Technique:

Before you begin, review the introduction to the Block and Wheel Cheeses on page 54. Gather all of your ingredients (*mise en place*).

Combine the dried minced onion and chives in a small dish and set aside.

Prepare the cheese according to the Preparation and Cooking Technique instructions on page 57. Stir in the onion and chives while cooking the cheese.

"I live in Somerset, in England, about 10 miles from Cheddar and about 30 miles from Gloucestershire. The other day I gave my farmer neighbour some of the non-dairy Gloucester with Onions and Chives to try. He's just been in to tell me he can't stop thinking about it, and can't believe I can make such an authentic tasting cheese in my own kitchen, all without the aid of a single cow!" ...Lois Martin

Tofu-Based Cheeses

Sharp Tofu Cheddar

This recipe produces a sharp, solid cheddar without culturing. However, since the miso used in the recipe is a "living food", it does contribute to some degree of ripening as the cheese firms and ages in the refrigerator.

Sharp tofu cheddar is a cold-snacking cheese, which means that although it will soften when heated, it will not melt in the same manner as the block cheeses. Slices are wonderful for serving on crackers or cold sandwiches. Sharp tofu cheddar can also be finely shredded and is ideal for topping foods where melting is not necessary or desirable, such as for topping tacos, taco salads or tostadas. Be sure to use **extra-firm** water-packed block tofu for the proper dry, crumbly texture. A food processor is recommended for efficient processing.

For this cheese you will need a glass, ceramic, metal or BPA-free plastic container which will hold a minimum of 2 cups liquid; this will act as the form to shape the cheese. Line the form with plastic wrap, leaving plenty of excess hanging over the sides. This will help lift the cheese from the form after firming. This recipe yields about 8 ounces.

Ingredients:

- ½ block (7 oz before pressing) extra-firm water-packed tofu (not silken tofu)
- ½ cup organic **refined** coconut oil
- ¾ cup water
- 1 T agar powder
- ¼ cup nutritional yeast flakes
- 2 T tomato paste or 1 T tomato powder
- 1 tsp lactic acid powder or 4 tsp fresh lemon juice
- 2 tsp raw apple cider vinegar
- ¾ tsp fine sea salt or kosher salt
- ¾ tsp onion powder
- ½ tsp dry ground mustard
- 2 T mellow white miso paste

Technique:

Press the tofu until it is not releasing any more liquid. It is important that the tofu be as dry as possible. To do this quickly, wrap the tofu in a lint-free kitchen towel and squeeze to remove the water. Crumble the tofu into a food processor and set aside.

Remove the lid from the jar of coconut oil and place the jar in a microwave. Heat until the solid oil liquefies, about 30 seconds to 1 minute (this will depend upon the solidity of the coconut oil). Alternately, you can place the jar in about an inch of simmering water and melt the oil in the same manner. Set aside.

Add the agar powder to the water in a small saucepan, stir and place over medium heat to bring to a simmer.

Meanwhile, add the remaining ingredients to the food processor, **except** for the miso. Add ½ cup of the melted coconut oil. Do not process yet.

When the agar mixture has come to a vigorous simmer, immediately pour into the food processor and process until the mixture is nearly smooth. Add the miso and continue to process until smooth. Stop to scrape down the sides of the processor bowl as necessary with a flexible spatula.

The cheese will begin to set as it cools, so immediately transfer the mixture to the form. Smooth the surface as best as you can with the back of a spoon.

Cover the form with plastic wrap, making sure the wrap comes into contact with the surface of the cheese. Use your fingers to further smooth the cheese surface through the plastic. Refrigerate a minimum of 8 hours or until very firm.

Once firmed, lift the cheese from the container. Wrap the cheese snugly in a paper towel and then wrap tightly in plastic wrap or seal in a zip-lock bag. Refrigerate for 24 hours. The paper towel will absorb any moisture released from the cheese during refrigeration and contribute to a firmer, drier texture.

The cheese is now ready to be sliced or shredded as needed and will continue to develop flavor as it ages.

Mediterranean Herbed Feta

This tofu-based cheese is simple to make and is reminiscent of dairy feta cheese in both taste and texture. It has a very tangy, salty flavor and is wonderful for topping Mediterranean salads, pizza or for using in recipes such as Greek Spanakopita.

For this cheese you will need a glass, ceramic, metal or BPA-free plastic container which will hold a minimum of 1 and ½ cup liquid; this will act as the form to shape the cheese. A food processor is recommended for efficient processing. This recipe yields about 8 ounces.

Ingredients:

- ½ block (7 oz) extra-firm water-packed tofu (not silken tofu)
- ¼ cup organic **refined** coconut oil
- 1 tsp lactic acid powder or 4 tsp fresh lemon juice
- 1 T white wine vinegar or raw apple cider vinegar
- 1 and ½ tsp fine sea salt or kosher salt
- ¼ tsp onion powder
- 1 tsp dried basil
- ½ tsp dried marjoram
- ½ tsp dried oregano

Technique:

Line the form with plastic wrap or a double-layer of cheesecloth, allowing some excess to hang over the sides. This will help lift the cheese from the container after firming.

Drain and press the tofu until it is not releasing any more liquid. It is essential to dry the tofu as much as possible for the proper texture. Crumble the tofu into a food processor.

Remove the metal lid from the jar of coconut oil and place the jar in a microwave. Heat just until the solid oil liquefies, about 30 seconds to 1 minute (this will depend upon the solidity of the coconut oil). Alternately, place the jar in about an inch of simmering water and melt the oil in the same manner. Measure ¼ cup and add to the food processor with the remaining ingredients **except** for the dried herbs. Process the contents until very smooth.

Add the dried herbs and pulse to combine. Transfer the cheese mixture to the lined form. Pack the mixture with the back of a spoon and smooth the surface as best you can. Cover with plastic wrap and refrigerate for a minimum of 8 hours. This will ensure that the coconut oil has completely solidified. Once firmed, lift the cheese from the container and crumble as needed.

When using as a topping for salads, toss the salad first with the dressing and then add the crumbles. Cubed feta is wonderful drizzled with olive oil and served with falafel and other Mediterranean favorites. Store in a zip-lock bag or wrapped tightly in plastic wrap in the refrigerator.

Chèvre Soja
with Basil Pesto and Sundried Tomato

This tangy tofu-based chèvre is flavored with non-dairy basil pesto (traditional pesto includes dairy parmesan) and sun-dried tomatoes. It makes a flavorful spread for crackers or crusty bread. A food processor is recommended for efficient processing. This recipe yields about 8 ounces.

Ingredients:

- ½ block (7 oz) extra-firm water-packed tofu (not silken tofu)
- 3 T organic **refined** coconut oil
- 1 and ½ tsp lactic acid powder or 2 T fresh lemon juice
- 1 tsp fine sea salt or kosher salt
- ¼ tsp onion powder
- 2 T finely chopped sun-dried tomatoes (dry or oil-packed)
- 2 T Basil Pesto (recipe follows)

Technique:

Drain and press the tofu until it is not releasing any more liquid. It is essential to dry the tofu as much as possible for the proper texture. Crumble the tofu into a food processor.

Finely chop the sun-dried tomatoes (if the tomatoes were packed in oil, be sure to blot them thoroughly with a paper towel to remove the excess oil). Set aside.

Remove the metal lid from the jar of coconut oil and place the jar in a microwave. Heat just until the solid oil liquefies, about 30 seconds to 1 minute (this will depend upon the solidity of the coconut oil). Alternately, place the jar in about an inch of simmering water and melt the oil in the same manner. Measure 3 tablespoons and add to the food processor. Add the lactic acid powder or lemon juice and salt.

Process the contents until completely smooth. Transfer the mixture to a container with a lid, stir in the chopped sun-dried tomatoes and swirl in the pesto. Cover and refrigerate for a minimum of 8 hours.

After 8 hours, lay a sheet of plastic wrap onto a work surface and scoop the cheese mixture onto the wrap. With your fingers, gently form the cheese into a log shape. Don't worry about shaping perfection; the wrap will shape the cheese into a log when rolled. Roll the mixture inside the wrap and twist the ends tightly. Place the roll in the refrigerator for 1 hour to re-firm the cheese before serving.

Basil Pesto

Pesto is a sauce originating in Genoa in the northern region of Italy. The name is derived from the Italian *pestare*, which means to pound, or to crush, in reference to the original method of preparation with mortar and pestle. However, for the sake of convenience, pesto can be prepared in a food processor.

Ingredients:

- 5 cloves garlic
- ⅓ cup pine nuts or chopped walnuts
- 1 large bunch fresh basil leaves (about 2 cups)
- ⅓ cup olive oil
- ½ tsp coarse ground black pepper, or more to taste
- ¼ tsp fine sea salt or kosher salt, or more to taste
- ⅓ cup grated Hard Parmesan (pg. 97) or Grated Parmesan (pg. 99)

Technique:

Preheat the oven to 350°F. Place the garlic cloves on a baking sheet lined with foil and roast for 5 minutes. Remove the baking sheet from the oven and scatter the nuts in a single layer next to the garlic. Return to the oven and roast for 5 to 6 minutes until the nuts are lightly toasted; avoid over-browning. Remove from the oven and set aside to cool.

When cooled, add the garlic and nuts to a food processor and process until finely ground. Add the basil leaves, salt and pepper and process until puréed. While the processor is running, pour the olive oil into the mixture through the food chute and process for about 30 seconds. Stop the motor and add the parmesan. Process until combined. Add additional salt and pepper to taste as desired. The sauce will last in the refrigerator for about 1 week. Pesto does not require cooking before using in recipes.

Gorgonzola

Dairy gorgonzola is a variety of Italian blue cheese. It has a salty flavor and strong bite which is produced by the mold *Penicillium glaucum*. This mold also gives gorgonzola its characteristic blue-green veins. While this tofu-based version doesn't capture the pungent quality of dairy gorgonzola exactly, it has a tangy flavor that is wonderful when served on crackers or as a crumbled topping on salads, pizza, risotto or polenta. Be sure to use extra-firm water-packed block tofu for the proper dry, crumbly texture. A food processor is recommended for efficient processing.

For this cheese you will need a glass, ceramic, metal or BPA-free plastic container which will hold a minimum of 1 and ½ cup liquid; this will act as the form to shape the cheese. This recipe yields about 8 ounces.

Ingredients:

- ½ block (7 oz) extra-firm water-packed tofu (not silken tofu)
- ¼ cup organic **refined** coconut oil
- 2 T mellow white miso paste
- 4 tsp white wine or champagne vinegar
- ½ tsp lactic acid powder or 2 tsp fresh lemon juice
- 1 tsp fine sea salt or kosher salt
- ½ tsp onion powder
- ¼ tsp garlic powder
- ⅛ tsp blue-green algae powder (spirulina)

Technique:

Line the form with plastic wrap or a double-layer of cheesecloth, being sure to leave some excess hanging over the sides. This will help lift the cheese from the form after firming.

Drain and press the tofu until it is not releasing any more liquid. It is essential to dry the tofu as much as possible for the proper texture. Crumble the tofu into a food processor.

Remove the metal lid from the jar of coconut oil and place the jar in a microwave. Heat just until the solid oil liquefies, about 30 seconds to 1 minute (this will depend upon the solidity of the coconut oil). Alternately, place the jar in about an inch of simmering water and melt the oil in the same manner. Measure ¼ cup and add to the food processor with the remaining ingredients **except** for the algae powder. Process the contents until very smooth.

Transfer the cheese mixture to a bowl. Dot the cheese in several spots with the algae powder and fold (rather than stir) the cheese over a few times to create swirls of blue-green color. Transfer the cheese to the lined form. Pack the mixture with the back of a spoon and smooth the surface as best you can. Cover with plastic wrap and refrigerate for a minimum of 8 hours. This will ensure that the coconut oil has completely solidified.

Lift the cheese from the container and slice or crumble as needed. Store the cheese wrapped in plastic wrap or in a zip-lock bag in the refrigerator. Because this cheese is made with miso, a fermented product, the flavor will continue to develop as it ages.

Gorgonzola, Pear and Candied Walnut Salad

Fresh greens, sliced pears, candied walnuts and crumbled, tangy Gorgonzola are dressed with a light and fresh vinaigrette which highlights the sweet and savory flavors of the classic salad. This recipe yields about 4 to 6 servings.

Ingredients:

- ⅔ cup champagne vinegar, white balsamic vinegar or white wine vinegar
- 1 T light brown sugar
- 1 teaspoon Dijon mustard
- 1 shallot, minced or 3 T minced red onion
- ⅞ cup (¾ cup plus 2 T) olive oil
- 2 T roasted walnut oil (or additional olive oil)
- ½ tsp sea salt or kosher salt, or more to taste
- ½ tsp coarse ground black pepper, or more to taste
- 8 cups washed and torn lettuces and/or mixed greens
- 3 pears, peeled, cored, and sliced
- 1 and ½ cup candied walnuts (recipe follows)
- 8 oz Gorgonzola (pg. 88) or Bleu Cheese (pg. 52)

Technique:

In a small bowl whisk together the vinegar, sugar, mustard, salt, pepper and shallot until smooth. Slowly add the oils, whisking constantly, until emulsified. Taste and add salt and pepper as desired. The dressing can be stored in an airtight container and refrigerated for up to two days prior to serving. Mix well before using.

In a large bowl toss together the lettuces/greens with the dressing, reserving about three tablespoons of the dressing. Place the greens on individual serving plates and top with a fan of pear slices. Sprinkle the candied walnuts and crumble the cheese over the salads. Drizzle the remaining dressing over top each of plate and serve immediately.

For the candied walnuts you will need:

- ⅓ cup organic sugar
- 1 and ½ cup raw walnut pieces
- ¼ tsp sea salt or kosher salt

Technique:

Preheat the oven to 350°F. Spread the walnuts on a baking sheet in a single layer. Bake for 5 minutes on a middle rack. Test for doneness. If not quite toasted enough, toast for 1 or 2 more minutes. Be careful not to burn. Remove from the oven and let cool.

Pour the sugar into a small saucepan. Have the walnuts nearby, ready to quickly add to the pan at the proper time. Cook the sugar over medium heat, stirring with a wooden spoon until the sugar begins to melt. Keep stirring until all the sugar has melted and the color reaches medium amber. As soon as sugar is melted and the color is medium amber, add the walnuts to the pan, quickly stirring and coating each piece with the sugar mixture. Spread the sugar-coated walnuts on a rimmed baking sheet, lined either with a silicone non-stick mat or parchment paper. Use two forks to separate the walnuts from each other, working very quickly (if some of the nuts are clumped together, don't worry, they can be separated once completely cooled). Sprinkle the nuts with the salt. Let cool completely.

Queso Fresco

Queso Fresco is a soft, creamy, mildly tangy and crumbly Mexican cheese which is widely used in Mexican and Tex-Mex cuisine. This tofu-based version is simple to make and is reminiscent of dairy queso fresco in both taste and texture. Be sure to use extra-firm water-packed block tofu for the proper soft, crumbly texture. A food processor is recommended for efficient processing.

For this cheese you will need a glass, ceramic, metal or BPA-free plastic container which will hold a minimum of 1 and ½ cup liquid; this will act as the form to shape the cheese. This recipe yields about 8 ounces.

Ingredients:

- ½ block (7 oz) extra-firm water-packed tofu (not silken tofu)
- ¼ cup organic **refined** coconut oil
- ¼ cup plain unsweetened non-dairy milk*
- ¾ tsp lactic acid powder
- ¾ tsp fine sea salt or kosher salt

*Homemade almond or cashew milk is ideal because of its creamy consistency and ability to minimize the chalky undertaste of the tofu.

Technique:

Line the form with a double-layer of cheesecloth or plastic wrap with plenty of excess hanging over the edges; set aside.

Drain and press the tofu until it is not releasing any more liquid. It is essential to dry the tofu as much as possible for the proper texture. Crumble the tofu into a food processor.

Remove the metal lid from the jar of coconut oil and place the jar in a microwave. Heat just until the solid oil liquefies, about 30 seconds to 1 minute (this will depend upon the solidity of the coconut oil). Alternately, place the jar in about an inch of simmering water and melt the oil in the same manner. Measure ¼ cup and add to the food processor with the remaining ingredients. Process the contents until very smooth.

Transfer the cheese mixture to the lined container. Pack the mixture with the back of a spoon and smooth the surface as best you can. Cover with plastic wrap and refrigerate for a minimum of 8 hours. This will ensure that the coconut oil has completely solidified. Lift the cheese from the container and crumble as needed. Store the cheese wrapped in plastic wrap or in a zip-lock bag in the refrigerator.

Creamy Ricotta
with Optional Herbs

Creamy ricotta is superb for stuffed pasta shells, manicotti or lasagna. Homemade almond milk or cashew milk is ideal for lightening the flavor and texture of the tofu, yielding a mild and creamy cheese with a subtle hint of sweetness that is present in dairy ricotta. The herbs are optional and variations are provided for creating spinach or pesto ricotta. This recipe yields about 2 cups.

Ingredients:

- 1 block (14 oz) firm or extra-firm water-packed tofu (not silken tofu)
- ¾ cup plain unsweetened non-dairy milk (homemade nut milk is ideal)
- 2 T olive oil
- ½ tsp lactic acid powder or 2 tsp fresh lemon juice
- 1 tsp nutritional yeast flakes
- ½ tsp fine sea salt or kosher salt
- ¼ tsp ground white pepper
- 1 tsp each of dried basil, parsley, and oregano (optional)

Technique:

Drain and press the tofu until it is not releasing any more liquid. It is essential to dry the tofu as much as possible for the proper texture.

Crumble the tofu into a food processor (or alternately mash the tofu in a mixing bowl with a fork). Add the soymilk and remaining ingredients and process (or stir) until the tofu is nearly smooth but still retains some texture. Stir in the optional dried herbs.

Alternately, you can stir in ¼ cup prepared Basil Pesto (pg. 87) or follow the directions for creating Spinach Ricotta on the following page.

Use small amounts of additional soymilk to thin to desired consistency as needed. Refrigerate in a covered container until ready to use.

Spinach Ricotta

Thaw a 10-ounce package of frozen spinach. Press the spinach in a fine-mesh strainer using the back of large spoon (alternately use a tofu press or squeeze dry in a clean kitchen towel) to remove as much moisture as possible. Add the spinach to a food processor and pulse to finely chop. Add the chopped spinach to the ricotta in a bowl and stir to blend. Spinach ricotta is delicious in stuffed pasta shells, manicotti and lasagna.

For stuffed pasta shells, boil the shells in salted water according to the package directions. Drain in a colander. When the shells are cool enough to handle, stuff them with the ricotta and place in an oiled baking dish. Top with grated mozzarella, and parmesan if desired, and bake at 350°F until the cheese is nicely melted.

Baked Manicotti

Tender manicotti shells are filled with a mixture of non-dairy Basil Pesto and creamy Ricotta cheese, topped with marinara sauce, Mozzarella Fior di Latte cheese and grated Hard Parmesan and then baked to perfection.

Ingredients:

- 1 and ½ cup Chef's Best Marinara Sauce (recipe follows) or commercial marinara sauce
- 1 recipe Creamy Ricotta (pg. 91)
- 1 cup Mozzarella Fior di Latte, shredded (pg. 60)
- ¼ cup grated Hard Parmesan (pg. 97)
- optional: ¼ cup Basil Pesto (pg. 87)*
- 6 manicotti, cooked, rinsed in cold water
- coarse ground black pepper, to taste

*The basil pesto is optional; if you prefer you can prepare the ricotta with spinach instead according to the directions in the ricotta recipe; or simply omit the pesto or spinach altogether.

Technique:

Prepare the marinara sauce, cheeses and optional pesto in advance.

Cook the manicotti according to the package directions (generally about 7 minutes in boiling salted water - do not overcook!). Rinse with cold water and set aside to drain.

Preheat the oven to 350°F.

Spread ¾ cup of the marinara sauce on the bottom of 13 x 9-inch baking dish.

If using the pesto, stir the pesto into the ricotta. Spoon the ricotta mixture into a large re-sealable plastic bag. With scissors, cut a small hole from one of the bottom corners of the bag (alternately, a pastry bag can be used for piping the filling into the shells).

Fill the manicotti shells, 1 at a time, by squeezing the ricotta mixture into both sides of each shell. Place the filled manicotti over the sauce in the baking dish; pour the remaining ¾ cup marinara sauce over the manicotti. Top with the shredded mozzarella and grated parmesan and season with black pepper to taste. Cover with foil and bake for 45 minutes. Remove the foil and serve immediately.

Chef's Best Marinara Sauce

Ingredients:

- 2 T olive oil
- 1 medium onion, diced
- 3 cloves minced garlic
- 1 can (28 oz.) crushed tomatoes
  or 2 lbs vine-ripened tomatoes, peeled* and crushed
- ¼ cup dry white wine (e.g., Chardonnay, Sauvignon Blanc)
- 2 T tomato paste
- 1 T organic sugar
- 1 tsp sea salt or kosher salt
- 1 tsp dried basil or 1 T fresh basil, finely minced
- 1 tsp dried oregano or 1 T fresh oregano, finely minced
- ¼ tsp coarse ground black pepper, or more to taste

*To peel fresh tomatoes, blanch them by immersing them in boiling water for 1 minute. Immediately immerse them in an ice-water bath. The skins should slip off easily. Pulse the tomatoes a few times in a food processor to crush.

Technique:

In a large saucepan, sauté the onions in olive oil over medium heat until translucent. Add the garlic and sauté an additional 2 minutes.

Add the crushed tomatoes, tomato paste, white wine, sugar, salt, herbs and pepper. The sugar is important, as it tempers the acidity of the tomatoes, so do not omit unless you are diabetic. Bring to a simmer, cover and reduce the heat to just above low. Cook for about 45 minutes and season with additional salt and pepper as desired. The marinara sauce is now ready to use.

Cottage Cheese

This creamy non-dairy cottage cheese is very similar in both taste and texture to its dairy counterpart. Try stirring in some drained pineapple tidbits; or try minced fresh chives for a savory flavor. This recipe yields about 16 ounces of cottage cheese.

Ingredients:

- 1 block (14 oz) firm or extra-firm water-packed tofu (not silken tofu)
- ¾ cup plain unsweetened non-dairy milk* plus additional for moistening as needed
- ⅓ cup No-Eggy Mayo (pg. 140)
- ½ tsp fine sea salt or kosher salt

*Homemade almond or cashew milk is ideal because of its creamy consistency and ability to minimize the chalky undertaste of the tofu.

Technique:

Press the tofu to remove as much moisture as possible. In a mixing bowl, mash the tofu with a fork but leave a little texture. Set aside.

Add the milk, mayonnaise and salt and mix thoroughly (if the tofu seems a bit saucy at first, don't worry, it will absorb a substantial amount of moisture after several minutes).

Refrigerate for a few hours to chill before serving. If the cottage cheese appears dry after chilling, stir in small amounts of additional milk to moisten to the desired consistency.

Garlic Herb Gournay

This garlicky, semi-soft cheese makes a flavorful spread for crackers or crusty bread. The texture is similar to Boursin™, a trademarked brand of Gournay cheese. A food processor is recommended for efficient processing. This recipe yields about 8 ounces.

Ingredients:

- ½ block (7 oz) extra-firm water-packed tofu (not silken tofu)
- 3 T organic **refined** coconut oil
- ¾ tsp lactic acid powder or 1 T fresh lemon juice
- 1 tsp white wine vinegar or raw apple cider vinegar
- 1 to 2 cloves garlic, chopped
- 2 tsp dried parsley
- 2 tsp dried minced chives
- 1 tsp dried basil
- 1 tsp fine sea salt or kosher salt
- ½ tsp onion powder
- ½ tsp coarse ground black pepper
- ¼ tsp dried thyme leaves
- plain unsweetened non-dairy milk to adjust consistency as needed*

*Homemade almond or cashew milk is ideal because of its creamy consistency and ability to minimize the chalky undertaste of the tofu.

Technique:

Press the tofu to remove as much moisture as possible and then crumble into a food processor.

Remove the metal lid from the jar of coconut oil and place the jar in a microwave. Heat just until the solid oil liquefies, about 30 seconds to 1 minute (this will depend upon the solidity of the coconut oil). Alternately, place the jar in about an inch of simmering water and melt the oil in the same manner. Measure 3 tablespoons and add to the food processor with the remaining ingredients. Process the contents until very smooth.

Transfer the mixture to a container with a lid. Cover and refrigerate for a minimum of 6 hours to allow the flavors to blend and the cheese to firm. If desired, transfer the cheese to a decorative container and allow the cheese to soften for about 15 minutes at room temperature before serving. Gournay should be thick, yet spreadable. If the cheese is dry and crumbly, stir in small amounts of non-dairy milk until the desired consistency is achieved.

Zesty Onion Dill Gournay

This savory, semi-soft cheese is bursting with onion and fresh dill flavor and makes a wonderful spread for crackers or crusty bread. The texture is similar to Boursin™, a trademarked brand of Gournay cheese. A food processor is recommended for efficient processing. This recipe yields about 8 ounces.

Ingredients:

- ½ block (7 oz) extra-firm water-packed tofu (not silken tofu)
- 3 T organic **refined** coconut oil
- 1 T prepared horseradish (not creamed)
- ¾ tsp lactic acid powder or 1 T fresh lemon juice
- 1 tsp white wine vinegar or raw apple cider vinegar
- 1 tsp fine sea salt or kosher salt
- ½ tsp garlic powder
- ¼ tsp ground white pepper
- 2 T fresh minced dill
- 1 T dried minced onion
- plain unsweetened non-dairy milk to adjust consistency as needed*

*Homemade almond or cashew milk is ideal because of its creamy consistency and ability to minimize the chalky undertaste of the tofu.

Technique:

Press the tofu to remove as much moisture as possible and then crumble into a food processor.

Remove the metal lid from the jar of coconut oil and place the jar in a microwave. Heat just until the solid oil liquefies, about 30 seconds to 1 minute (this will depend upon the solidity of the coconut oil). Alternately, place the jar in about an inch of simmering water and melt the oil in the same manner. Measure 3 tablespoons and add to the food processor with the remaining ingredients **except** for the dill and dried onion. Process the contents until very smooth.

Transfer the mixture to a container with a lid and stir in the dill and dried onion. Cover and refrigerate for a minimum of 6 hours to allow the flavors to blend and the cheese to firm. If desired, transfer the cheese to a decorative container and allow the cheese to soften for about 15 minutes at room temperature before serving. Gournay should be thick, yet spreadable. If the cheese is dry and crumbly, stir in small amounts of non-dairy milk until the desired consistency is achieved.

Miscellaneous Cheeses

Hard Parmesan

Hard Parmesan is a golden, hard cheese with a granular texture reminiscent of dairy Parmesan. While it lacks the "stinky" odor component of dairy parmesan, it has its own unique identity and savory flavor which will complement any dish calling for parmesan. It can be shaved, crumbled or grated and it will melt in hot foods. Because this parmesan is made with miso, a fermented product or "living" food, the flavor will continue to develop as it ages. It will also stay fresh in the refrigerator for several weeks or more if stored in an airtight container (and possibly months). A food processor is required for this recipe; do not use a blender. The raw cashews should not be pre-soaked for this recipe.

Ingredients:

- 1 and ½ cup (7.5 oz) whole raw cashews
- 2 T organic **refined** coconut oil
- 1 T nutritional yeast flakes
- 1 T mellow white miso paste
- 1 tsp raw apple cider vinegar
- ¾ tsp lactic acid powder
- ½ tsp fine sea salt or kosher salt
- ½ tsp onion powder
- ¼ tsp garlic powder

Tip: If you are allergic to soy, look for miso paste made from barley or chickpeas.

Technique:

Line a 2-cup minimum glass, ceramic, metal or plastic form with plastic wrap, leaving excess hanging over the sides. Alternately, line the bottom of the form with parchment paper. This will aid removal of the cheese once it has hardened.

Remove the metal lid from the jar of coconut oil and place the jar in a microwave. Heat just until the solid oil liquefies, about 30 seconds to 1 minute (this will depend upon the solidity of the coconut oil). Alternately, place the jar in about an inch of simmering water and melt the oil in the same manner.

Add the dry cashews to a food processor and pulse as many times as necessary to grind into coarse flour.

Add the remaining ingredients, including 2 tablespoons of the melted coconut oil, and process until crumbly, about 1 full minute. Firmly pack the cheese mixture into the form using the back of a spoon.

Place a piece of plastic wrap over the surface of the cheese and smooth the surface with your fingers. Refrigerate for a minimum of 8 hours or until very hard. Use the plastic wrap to help remove the cheese from its form. If it won't release easily (and it probably won't), gently pry it loose with a table knife. If the surface of the cheese feels oily, blot with a paper towel. Grate or shave as needed and keep stored in an airtight container or a zip-lock bag in the refrigerator. The flavor will continue to develop as the cheese ages.

Garlic Parmesan Crostini

Technique:

Preheat the oven to 325°F.

Slice a loaf of crusty Italian or French bread ¼-inch thick on the bias (diagonal).

Crush and finely mince 2 cloves of garlic. Mix the garlic with ¼ cup olive oil.

Brush each bread slice with the olive oil/garlic mixture and place the slices in a single layer on a baking sheet.

Sprinkle the slices with shaved Hard Parmesan (pg. 97) and bake until golden brown.

Risotto Parmesan

Risotto is an Italian rice dish prepared from high-starch, short grain rice that has been cooked in a seasoned stock or broth to a creamy consistency.

Ingredients:

- 1 quart (4 cups) Golden Stock (pg. 79)
- 1 and ½ cup Arborio rice
- ½ cup dry white wine
- 1 small leek, white and light green parts only, split and rinsed to remove any sand and then chopped
- 3 T Better Butter (pg. 28) or Vital Butter (pg. 33)
- 1 T olive oil
- ¼ cup shaved Hard Parmesan (pg. 97)
- sea salt or kosher salt, to taste

Technique:

Bring the stock to a simmer in a medium saucepan and then reduce the heat to low. In a large saucepan, heat the oil and 1 tablespoon butter over medium heat. When the butter has melted, add the chopped leek and sauté for 2-3 minutes.

Add the rice and stir briskly with a wooden spoon so that the grains are coated with the oil and melted butter. Sauté for another minute or two until the rice emits a nutty aroma, but do not brown. Add the wine and cook while stirring, until the liquid is fully absorbed.

Add a ladle of hot stock to the rice and stir until the liquid is fully absorbed. When the rice appears almost dry, add another ladle of stock and repeat the process. Constant stirring is important while the stock is being added! Continue adding hot stock and stirring until the liquid is absorbed. As the rice cooks, it will release its natural starches and develop a creamy consistency.

Continue stirring and adding stock, a ladle at a time, for about 20 minutes or until the grains are "al dente" (tender but still firm to the bite), without being crunchy. Stir in the remaining 2 tablespoons butter and the parmesan; season with salt to taste.

Note: Risotto becomes glutinous if held for too long, so it should be served immediately. A properly cooked risotto should form a soft, creamy mound on a dinner plate; it shouldn't be stiff nor run across the plate.

Grated Parmesan

Grated Parmesan is very easy to make and has a granular texture reminiscent of dairy Parmesan. While it lacks the "stinky" odor component of dairy parmesan, it has its own unique identity and savory flavor which will complement any dish calling for parmesan.

Because this parmesan is made with miso, a fermented product or "living" food, the flavor will continue to develop during refrigeration. It will also stay fresh in the refrigerator for several weeks or more if stored in an airtight container. Grated Parmesan won't melt, so opt for Hard Parmesan (pg. 97) for foods that require a "melting" parmesan.

Ingredients:

- 1 cup almond meal
- 1 T nutritional yeast flakes
- 1 T mellow white miso paste
- ¾ tsp lactic acid powder
- ½ tsp fine sea salt or kosher salt
- ½ tsp onion powder
- ¼ tsp garlic powder

Technique:

Add all ingredients to a food processor and process until well-blended. Refrigerate the parmesan in a covered container until ready to use.

Tip: If you are allergic to soy, look for miso paste made from barley or chickpeas.

Italian Mascarpone

Italian mascarpone is an uncultured, spreadable dessert cheese made from whole raw cashews and soymilk. It resembles cream cheese although it is softer, with a pale cream color, light buttery flavor and a hint of natural sweetness. Italian Mascarpone is best known as an ingredient in the Italian dessert Tiramisu. Try it as a reduced-fat butter or cream cheese alternative for toast, bagels or muffins (there is no added oil in this recipe). A high-powered blender is recommended for efficient processing. This recipe yields about 16 ounces.

Ingredients:

- 1 and ½ cup (7.5 oz by weight) whole raw cashews
- 1 and ¼ cup pure soymilk (sorry, no substitutions)
- 2 tsp lactic acid powder*
- ½ tsp raw apple cider vinegar
- ¼ tsp fine sea salt or kosher salt

*Lactic acid powder can be replaced with an equal amount of citric acid powder, powdered Vitamin C (ascorbic acid), or 2 tablespoons plus 2 teaspoons fresh lemon juice; however, the finished flavor will be slightly different.

Technique:

Rinse the cashews to remove any dust or debris and drain thoroughly. In a covered container, soak the cashews in the soymilk for a minimum of 8 hours in the refrigerator. Add the cashews and soymilk to a high-powered blender and process the contents on high speed until completely smooth and creamy, stopping to scrape down the sides of the blender jar and push the mixture down into the blades as necessary (use a tamper tool if you have one).

Add the lactic acid, vinegar and salt and process until blended. Transfer the cheese mixture to a container with a lid and refrigerate until chilled and thickened.

Cheese Sauces

Gooey, creamy and delicious, cheese sauces wield the power to make just about any dish more delectable. The sauces were formulated using pure soymilk, therefore pure soymilk is recommended for achieving the proper consistency and stability. If you choose to use commercial soymilk with additives, or other non-dairy milks, expect variations in results.

The sauces were formulated with varying amounts of tapioca flour for thickening based upon my personal consistency preference and experience with the sauces in various cooking applications. To thin the consistency, whisk in additional soymilk. To thicken the consistency, sprinkle in additional tapioca starch while vigorously whisking and bring the sauce back to a gentle simmer until thickened.

Golden Cheddar Sauce

This velvety cheese sauce has a mild cheddar flavor that will please the entire family. It's ideal for preparing macaroni and cheese and cheesy rice.

Try pouring over freshly steamed vegetables or baked potatoes too. This recipe yields about 2 cups of sauce.

Ingredients:

- 1 and ¾ cup pure soymilk
- ¼ cup tapioca flour
- ¼ cup nutritional yeast flakes
- ¼ cup vegetable oil
- 1 T mellow white miso paste
- 1 T organic tomato paste or 1 and ½ tsp tomato powder
- 1 tsp fine sea salt or kosher salt, or more to taste
- 1 tsp raw apple cider vinegar
- ½ tsp dry ground mustard
- ½ tsp onion powder
- ¼ tsp lactic acid powder or 1 tsp fresh lemon juice
- ⅛ tsp garlic powder

Technique:

Whisk the ingredients together in a small saucepan until smooth. Place over medium-low heat and stir slowly and continually with a flexible spatula until the mixture becomes thickened, smooth and glossy. Please note that the golden color will develop as the cheese sauce cooks. Taste and add salt as desired and/or additional soymilk to lighten the consistency to your preference. Reduce the heat to low to keep warm until ready to serve, stirring occasionally.

Classic Mac' and Cheese

An American classic; creamy, cheesy comfort food at its finest!

Ingredients:

- 2 cups elbow macaroni
- salted water
- 2 cups Golden Cheddar Sauce (pg. 101)

Technique:

Prepare the macaroni according to package directions and cook until desired tenderness. While the macaroni is cooking, prepare the cheese sauce and keep warm over low heat, stirring occasionally.

Pour the macaroni from the cooking pot into a colander and shake to remove as much water as possible. Add the macaroni back to the warm cooking pot and toss thoroughly. The residual heat of the cooking pot will help evaporate any remaining water - this is very important or the water will dilute the cheese sauce! Stir in the cheese sauce.

At this point, you can transfer to a serving dish and serve immediately, or transfer the macaroni and cheese to a lightly oiled 8-inch baking dish and top with 2 tablespoons of fine dry breadcrumbs tossed with 2 teaspoons melted non-dairy butter. Broil for about 3 to 4 minutes or until golden brown on top; serve immediately.

Scalloped Potatoes Gratin

Sliced russet potatoes are baked in a luscious, Golden Cheddar Sauce until tender and delicious! Parboiling the potatoes briefly before baking ensures that the potato slices cook evenly in the gratin.

Ingredients:

- 2 lbs russet potatoes (about 4 large potatoes)
- 1 T Better Butter (pg. 28) or Vital Butter (pg. 33)
- 2 cups Golden Cheddar Sauce (pg. 101)
- ¼ tsp dried thyme
- sea salt or kosher salt and coarse ground black pepper to taste

Technique:

Peel the potatoes and slice them ⅛-inch thick. A mandoline makes the job much easier and creates more uniform slices - but watch your fingers! Place the slices immediately into a large pot of water to prevent the slices from oxidizing (turning brown). Add 2 teaspoons of salt, bring to a boil and cook for 1 minute.

Immediately remove from the heat and drain the slices in a colander. DO NOT rinse with water! The potatoes will continue to cook slightly as they cool in the colander. Drain well and then place the slices on several layers of paper towels or a clean lint-free kitchen towel on your work surface. Pat them dry with additional towels.

Preheat the oven to 375°F.

Prepare the cheese sauce and keep warm over low heat, stirring occasionally.

Next, grease a shallow casserole dish with the butter. Place a layer of potato slices in an overlapping pattern and season lightly with salt and pepper. Spoon a little of the cheese sauce over the potatoes and spread evenly.

Continue to layer the potatoes with a light sprinkle of salt and pepper and then the cheese sauce. Sprinkle the top with the dried thyme and bake uncovered for 45 minutes. If the top has not sufficiently browned, set the oven on "broil" and cook an additional 1 to 2 minutes. Watch carefully so they do not burn. Remove from the oven and serve.

Sauce Fromage Blanc

This smooth, mild and creamy white cheese sauce is superb for pouring over pasta, potatoes, vegetables or savory filled crêpes. This recipe yields about 2 cups of sauce.

Ingredients:

- 1 and ¾ cup pure soymilk
- ¼ cup mild vegetable oil
- 3 T tapioca flour
- 2 T dry sherry or dry white wine
- 2 T nutritional yeast flakes
- 1 T mellow white miso paste
- 1 T sesame tahini
- ½ tsp fine sea salt or kosher salt, or more to taste
- ¼ tsp ground coriander

*The sherry or wine can be omitted for health or ethical reasons, but this will alter the flavor profile.

Technique:

Whisk the ingredients together in a small saucepan until smooth. Place over medium-low heat and stir slowly and continually with a flexible spatula until the mixture becomes thickened, smooth and glossy. Please note that the golden color will develop as the cheese sauce cooks. Taste and add salt as desired and/or additional soymilk to lighten the consistency to your preference. Reduce the heat to low to keep warm until ready to serve, stirring occasionally.

Potatoes Dauphinoise

In the culinary arts, the French word *Dauphinoise* refers to a recipe in which potatoes are sliced, layered in a baking dish and then baked au gratin with garlic, butter, heavy cream, cheese (traditionally Gruyère or Swiss Emmental) and a hint of ground nutmeg. The name Dauphinoise comes from the Dauphiné region of France, where the recipe is said to have originated. Although the names are similar, Potatoes Dauphinoise is not the same recipe as Dauphine potatoes, which are balls of puréed potatoes mixed with choux pastry and then deep-fried until light and crispy.

For the non-dairy version of this dish, Sauce Fromage Blanc was chosen for its flavor, as well as its simplicity in preparation. The combination of the cheesy sauce with the moisture from the boiled potato slices creates a superb heavy cream and melted cheese texture.

Ingredients:

- 2 cloves garlic
- 2 and ½ lbs Yukon gold potatoes or russet potatoes
- 2 cups Sauce Fromage Blanc (pg. 104)
- ½ tsp ground white pepper
- 1 T Better Butter (pg. 28) or Vital Butter (pg. 33)
- ground nutmeg

Technique:

Cut the garlic cloves in half and rub the interior of a shallow casserole dish. Set the dish aside and save the garlic.

Peel the potatoes and slice them ⅛-inch thick. A mandoline makes the job much easier and creates more uniform slices - but watch your fingers! Place the slices immediately into a large pot of water to prevent the slices from oxidizing (turning brown). Add 2 teaspoons of salt and add the cut garlic. Bring to a boil and cook for exactly 3 minutes.

Remove from the heat and drain the slices in a colander. DO NOT rinse with cold water and do not pat the potatoes dry with paper towels! The potatoes will continue to cook slightly as they cool in the colander. Discard the garlic.

Preheat the oven to 400°F.

In the meantime, prepare the Sauce Fromage Blanc and stir in the white pepper. Taste and season with additional salt as desired; set aside over low heat to keep warm.

"Grease" the interior of the baking dish with the butter. Place a layer of potatoes in the bottom of the baking dish and pour some of the cheese sauce over the layer. Repeat layering with the potatoes and the sauce. Be sure to leave enough sauce to cover the top of the potatoes.

Very lightly dust the top of the potatoes with ground nutmeg. Bake uncovered for 45 minutes. If the top has not sufficiently browned, set the oven on "broil" and cook an additional 1 to 2 minutes. Watch carefully so the potatoes do not burn. Remove from the oven and serve.

Mornay Sauce

Mornay sauce traditionally consists of mild Béchamel sauce enriched with shredded Gruyère or Swiss cheese and sometimes grated parmesan. However, I've simplified the construction of the sauce into one step using non-dairy ingredients. Mornay sauce is an essential component of Eggless Eggs Mornay (pg. 133), and is also delightful served over fresh steamed vegetables or pasta. This recipe yields about 2 cups of sauce.

Ingredients:

- 1 and ¾ cups pure soymilk
- ¼ cup mild vegetable oil
- 3 T plus 1 tsp tapioca flour
- 2 T mellow white miso paste
- 1 T extra-dry vermouth
- 1 T nutritional yeast
- 1 tsp raw apple cider vinegar
- ½ tsp fine sea salt or kosher salt, or more to taste
- ¼ tsp dry ground mustard
- ⅛ tsp ground coriander
- ⅛ tsp ground nutmeg

*The vermouth can be omitted for health or ethical reasons, but this will alter the flavor profile.

Technique:

Whisk the ingredients together in a small saucepan until smooth. Place over medium-low heat and stir slowly and continually with a flexible spatula until the mixture becomes thickened, smooth and glossy. Please note that the golden color will develop as the cheese sauce cooks. Taste and add salt as desired. Reduce the heat to low to keep warm until ready to serve, stirring occasionally.

Queso Nacho Sauce

As the name implies, this Mexican-style cheese sauce is perfect for topping nachos. This recipe yields about 2 cups of sauce.

Ingredients:

- 1 and ¾ cup pure soymilk
- ¼ cup nutritional yeast flakes
- ¼ cup tapioca flour
- ¼ cup vegetable oil
- 1 T mellow white miso paste
- 2 tsp raw apple cider vinegar
- 1 tsp fine sea salt or kosher salt
- 1 tsp ancho chili powder
- ½ tsp onion powder
- ¼ tsp ground red pepper or cayenne pepper

Technique:

Whisk the ingredients together in a small saucepan until smooth. Place over medium-low heat and stir slowly and continually with a flexible spatula until the mixture becomes thickened, smooth and glossy. Please note that the golden color will develop as the cheese sauce cooks. Taste and add salt as desired and/or additional soymilk to lighten the consistency to your preference. Reduce the heat to low to keep warm until ready to serve, stirring occasionally.

Tip: For hot and cheesy nacho bean dip, heat 1 can (16 oz) vegetarian refried beans in a saucepan and stir in 1 cup queso nacho sauce. Garnish with pickled sliced jalapenos, diced onion and chopped cilantro, if desired.

Queso Blanco Sauce
(Mexican White Cheese Sauce)

This Mexican-style white cheese sauce is flavored with mild green chilies and is wonderful for dipping warm tortillas or tortilla chips, or for pouring over your favorite Mexican or Tex-Mex foods. This recipe yields about 2 cups of sauce.

Ingredients:

- 1 and ¾ cup pure soymilk
- ¼ cup mild vegetable oil
- 3 T tapioca flour
- 1 T nutritional yeast flakes
- 2 tsp raw apple cider vinegar
- 1 tsp ground cumin
- 1 tsp fine sea salt or kosher salt
- 1 can (4 oz) diced mild green chilies
- 2 T finely minced onion
- garnish: 1 to 2 T chopped fresh cilantro (optional)

Technique:

Process the ingredients **except** for the chilies, minced onion and cilantro in a blender on low speed until smooth. Transfer the mixture to a medium saucepan, add the chilies and minced onion and cook over medium-low heat, stirring slowly and continually with a flexible spatula until the mixture becomes thickened, smooth and glossy. Taste and add salt as desired and/or additional soymilk to lighten the consistency to your preference. Reduce the heat to low to keep warm until ready to serve, stirring occasionally. Garnish with the optional cilantro before serving if desired.

Salsa con Queso

Zesty and cheesy Salsa con Queso is wonderful served as a dip with tortilla chips or warm tortillas. It can also be used as a topping for your favorite Mexican and Tex-Mex dishes. This recipe yields about 2 cups of sauce.

Ingredients:

- ¾ cup pure soymilk
- ¼ cup nutritional yeast flakes
- ¼ cup vegetable oil
- ¼ cup tapioca flour
- ½ tsp onion powder
- ½ tsp fine sea salt or kosher salt
- ½ tsp garlic powder
- ¼ tsp ancho chili powder
- 1 cup red tomato salsa of your choice

Technique:

Place all ingredients **except** for the salsa in a blender and process on low speed until smooth. Transfer the mixture to a medium saucepan, add the salsa and cook the mixture over medium-low heat, stirring slowly and continually with a flexible spatula until the mixture becomes thickened, smooth and glossy. Please note that the golden color will develop as the cheese cooks. Taste and add salt as desired and/or additional soymilk to lighten the consistency to your preference. Reduce the heat to low to keep warm until ready to serve or keep warm in a mini crock pot or heated chafing dish, stirring occasionally.

Cheese Melts

As the name implies, the cheese melts have the consistency of, well... melted cheese. They're very similar to the block cheeses but with the omission of the carrageenan for firming. The cheese melts are ideal for spreading on sandwiches before grilling; as a filling for eggless egg omelets; or for stirring into any recipe where a uniformly melted cheese is desired, such as in mashed potatoes or casseroles (uniform melting is a common problem with many commercial non-dairy cheeses).

The cheese melts were formulated using pure soymilk, therefore pure soymilk is recommended for achieving the proper consistency and stability. If you choose to use commercial soymilk with additives or other non-dairy milks, expect variations in results. A small amount of food gum is added to increase viscosity and impart a slight stretch to the melt.

The melts can be prepared and used immediately in recipes or refrigerated for later use, which makes them very convenient. Any unused portions should be refrigerated in a food storage container with a lid. When chilled, the cheese melts become very thick and sticky but will re-melt instantly when heated. Briefly reheat in a microwave or in a small saucepan over low heat until melted.

Colby Melt

Colby is a mellow, golden cheese which can best be described as having a very mild cheddar flavor. This melt is ideal for preparing Classic Grilled Cheese sandwiches (pg. 116). This recipe yields about 1 cup of melted cheese.

Ingredients:

- ¾ cup pure soymilk
- ¼ cup mild vegetable oil
- 3 T tapioca flour
- 2 T nutritional yeast flakes
- 1 T mellow white miso paste
- 1 T tomato paste or 1 and ½ tsp tomato powder
- ¼ tsp dry ground mustard
- ¼ tsp onion powder
- ¼ tsp fine sea salt or kosher salt
- ¼ tsp guar gum, sodium alginate or xanthan gum

Technique:

In a small saucepan, vigorously whisk together the ingredients until smooth. Cook the mixture over medium-low heat, stirring slowly and continually with a flexible spatula. The golden color will develop as the mixture cooks.

As the mixture thickens and curdles (forms lumps), begin stirring vigorously until the curds disappear and the cheese becomes very thick, smooth and glossy. Keep warm over low heat, stirring occasionally, until ready to use. For a spreadable consistency, remove from the heat and allow the melt to thicken.

Twice-Baked Cheesy Broccoli Potatoes

Baked potato shells are stuffed with a blend of mashed potato, broccoli and melted cheese and re-baked until golden brown on top. This recipe serves 2 to 4.

Ingredients:

- 2 extra-large russet potatoes
- 1 and ½ cup chopped broccoli florets (or try cauliflower)
- 1 cup Colby Melt (pg. 110) or Tangy Cheddar Melt (pg. 115)
- fine sea salt or kosher salt and coarse ground black pepper to taste

Technique:

Preheat the oven to 400°F. Thoroughly scrub and rinse the potatoes under running water. Blot dry. Deeply pierce the potatoes twice on each side. Rub the potatoes with a scant amount of vegetable oil and place them directly on a middle oven rack. Bake for 1 hour.

Remove the potatoes and let them cool until they can be handled comfortably without burning your hands. Reduce the oven heat to 350°F. While the potatoes are cooling, prepare the cheese melt and keep warm over low heat.

Lightly steam the broccoli florets, about 1 minute. For a quick and easy way to do this if you prefer, place the florets in a microwave-safe bowl, cover with a dampened paper towel and microwave for 1 minute.

Slice the potatoes in half lengthwise and scoop out the pulp into a mixing bowl. Be sure to leave a little bit of the potato around the shell for support. Mash the potato pulp with a potato masher or ricer. Add the cheese Melt and stir thoroughly. Fold in the broccoli florets and season with salt and pepper to taste. Stuff the potato halves with the potato mixture and place them on a baking sheet. Bake the stuffed potatoes for 30 minutes and then place them under the broiler for about 3 to 5 minutes until golden brown on top. Serve immediately.

Jarlsberg Melt

Jarlsberg shares flavor similarities with Swiss cheese and can best be described as mild, buttery and nutty with a hint of sweetness. This cheese also makes a wonderful melt for Classic Grilled Cheese sandwiches (pg. 116). Do not omit the ground coriander, even though only a small amount is needed, as it is essential to the flavor of this melt. This recipe yields about 1 cup of melted cheese.

Ingredients:

- ¾ cup pure soymilk
- ¼ cup mild vegetable oil
- 3 T tapioca flour
- 1 T nutritional yeast flakes
- 1 T dry sherry or dry white wine*
- 2 tsp mellow white miso paste
- ½ T (1 and ½ tsp) sesame tahini
- ¼ tsp fine sea salt or kosher salt
- ¼ tsp guar gum, sodium alginate or xanthan gum
- ⅛ tsp ground coriander

*The sherry or wine can be omitted for health or ethical reasons, but this will alter the flavor profile.

Technique:

In a small saucepan, vigorously whisk together the ingredients until smooth. Cook the mixture over medium-low heat, stirring slowly and continually with a flexible spatula. The golden color will develop as the mixture cooks.

As the mixture thickens and curdles (forms lumps), begin stirring vigorously until the curds disappear and the cheese becomes very thick, smooth and glossy. Keep warm over low heat, stirring occasionally, until ready to use. For a spreadable consistency, remove from the heat and allow the melt to thicken.

Käsespätzle
(German Spätzle with Cheese and Onions)

Ingredients:

- 1 recipe Spätzle (recipe follows)
- 2 T Better Butter (pg. 28) or Vital Butter (pg. 33)
- ½ cup diced onion
- 1 cup Jarlsberg Melt (pg. 112) or Gruyère Melt (pg. 118)
- sea salt or kosher salt and coarse ground black pepper to taste.

Technique:

Prepare the Spätzle batter and set aside. Place 3 quarts of water over high heat to bring to a rolling boil. Add 1 to 2 teaspoons of salt.

While the water is coming to a boil, prepare the Jarlsberg or Gruyère Melt according to directions. Keep warm over low heat.

Prepare the Spätzle according to the recipe directions. Remove to a large bowl and stir in 1 tablespoon butter as directed in the Spätzle recipe; set aside.

In a large skillet over medium heat, melt the remaining tablespoon of butter and sauté the onion until golden. Add the Spätzle to the skillet and toss thoroughly to heat through. Fold in the cheese melt. Add salt and black pepper to taste. Serve immediately.

Spätzle
German Dumplings

Spätzle are noodle-like German dumplings. Semolina flour is used in this recipe for the best flavor and texture. Semolina flour is ground from hard durum wheat. It has a sandy texture which works extremely well for making tender German dumplings and is also the flour of choice for handmade Italian pastas.

To form the Spätzle, you can use a traditional Spätzle maker or a Spätzle press. If you don't have either device, a standard colander with holes (not slots) will work too. This recipe yields about 4 to 6 servings.

Dry ingredients:

- 1 and ¼ cup semolina flour
- 1 and ½ tsp nutritional yeast flakes
- ½ tsp fine sea salt or kosher salt
- ¼ tsp kala namak (Himalayan black salt)
- ¼ tsp ground nutmeg
- ⅛ tsp ground white pepper

Liquid ingredients:

- 1 cup pure soymilk
- 1 T olive oil

Technique:

Whisk together the dry ingredients in a bowl. Add the soymilk and olive oil and whisk until a smooth and thick batter consistency is achieved.

Bring about 3 quarts of water to a rolling boil in a large pot. Add two teaspoons of salt.

Assorted devices for making Spätzle

Spray the Spätzle maker or press on both sides, including the little basket with cooking oil spray. If using a colander, spray the interior and exterior bottom of the basket. Spoon the batter into the basket.

If using a Spätzle maker, rest it over the pot of boiling water and slide the basket back and forth, thus dropping bits of batter into the water.

If using a press, add the mixture to the basket and gently press the batter, in increments, into the water. If using a colander, hold the basket handle with an oven mitt to protect from steam burns and press and scrape the batter through the holes in the bottom of the basket with a flexible spatula.

Cook the dumplings until they rise to the surface of the water (they cook quickly, about 1 to 2 minutes). Use a slotted spoon or pasta strainer ladle to collect the dumplings and place them in a bowl. Stir in 1 tablespoon non-dairy butter until melted. This will keep the Spätzle from sticking.

Tangy Cheddar Melt

Tangy Cheddar Melt has a sharp bite which makes it a lively alternative to the milder Colby. This recipe yields about 1 cup of melted cheese.

Ingredients:

- ¾ cup pure soymilk
- ¼ cup mild vegetable oil
- 3 T tapioca flour
- 2 T nutritional yeast flakes
- 1 T mellow white miso paste
- 1 tsp tomato paste or ½ tsp tomato powder*
- 1 tsp raw apple cider vinegar
- ½ tsp onion powder
- ½ tsp lactic acid powder or 2 tsp fresh lemon juice
- ¼ tsp dry ground mustard
- ¼ tsp guar gum, sodium alginate or xanthan gum

*For tangy, melted white cheddar, omit the tomato paste or powder.

Technique:

In a small saucepan, vigorously whisk together the ingredients until smooth. Cook the mixture over medium-low heat, stirring slowly and continually with a flexible spatula. The golden color will develop as the mixture cooks.

As the mixture thickens and curdles (forms lumps), begin stirring vigorously until the curds disappear and the cheese becomes very thick, smooth and glossy. Keep warm over low heat, stirring occasionally, until ready to use. For a spreadable consistency, remove from the heat and allow the melt to thicken.

Classic Grilled Cheese

Cheese Melts are ideal for preparing grilled cheese sandwiches since the cheese is already melted. If desired, other fillings can be added such as vegan deli slices, vegan bacon, sliced tomato and/or avocado slices. Each Cheese Melt recipe will yield about 1 cup of melted cheese, which should be enough for 3 to 4 sandwiches.

Ingredients:

- Cheese Melt of your choice
- Better Butter (pg. 28) or Vital Butter (pg. 33), room temperature
- sliced bread of your choice
- additional fillings of your choice

Technique:

Butter one side of all the bread slices. Spread the cheese on the non-buttered side of half of the bread slices. Layer with any additional fillings and top with the remaining slices of bread, butter side out. Place the sandwiches in a skillet over medium heat. Grill until golden brown on each side. Slice in half and serve.

Cheesy Broccoli and Cauliflower Rice Casserole

Ingredients:

- 1 T Better Butter (pg. 28) or Vital Butter (pg. 33)
- 1 cup uncooked rice of your choice
- Golden Stock (pg. 79), commercial vegan "chicken" broth or vegetable broth*
- ½ medium onion, diced
- 2 cups mixed and chopped broccoli and cauliflower
- Colby Melt (pg. 110) or Tangy Cheddar Melt (pg. 115)
- additional soymilk to adjust consistency as desired
- sea salt or kosher salt and coarse ground black pepper, to taste

*The amount of stock or broth required will depend upon the rice being used. Follow the package instructions and use the appropriate amount.

Technique:

In a large saucepan, bring the broth or water to a boil. Add the butter or margarine, rice and onion. Stir well, cover, reduce heat to a simmer and cook for the amount of time suggested on the rice package.

Meanwhile, while the rice is cooking, prepare your cheese melt and set aside. Preheat the oven to 350°F.

During the last 5 minutes of cooking time for the rice, add the vegetables on top of the rice and replace the lid. Do not stir! The vegetables will steam while the rice completes cooking.

Stir the cheese melt into the rice/vegetable mixture and season with salt and pepper to taste. If the mixture seems a bit dry, thoroughly stir in small amounts of soymilk in increments until the desired consistency is reached.

Transfer the mixture to a lightly oiled casserole dish, cover and bake for 30 minutes.

Uncover the casserole dish, set the oven on broil and lightly brown the top of the cheesy rice mixture under the broiler, about 5 minutes. Serve immediately.

Gruyère Melt

Dairy Gruyère is a slightly salty, ripened Swiss cheese. While its texture and complex flavor is difficult to reproduce in non-dairy form, this instant cheese melt captures the flavor of melted Gruyère fairly well, while retaining its own unique character. Do not omit the ground coriander, even though only a small amount is needed, as it is essential to the flavor of this melt.

Gruyère Melt is ideal for spreading on crusty bread to top French Onion Soup (pg. 120) before placing under the broiler. Stir Gruyère Melt into mashed potatoes to add flavor and creaminess (see Gruyère and Chive Mashed Potatoes, pg. 119). This recipe yields about 1 cup of melted cheese.

Ingredients:

- ¾ cup pure soymilk
- ¼ cup mild vegetable oil
- 3 T tapioca flour
- 2 T mellow white miso paste
- 1 T nutritional yeast flakes
- 1 T extra-dry vermouth
- 1 tsp raw apple cider vinegar
- ¼ tsp fine sea salt or kosher salt
- ¼ tsp dry ground mustard
- ¼ tsp guar gum, sodium alginate or xanthan gum
- ⅛ tsp ground coriander

*The vermouth can be omitted for health or ethical reasons, but this will alter the flavor profile.

Technique:

In a small saucepan, vigorously whisk together the ingredients until smooth. Cook the mixture over medium-low heat, stirring slowly and continually with a flexible spatula. The golden color will develop as the mixture cooks.

As the mixture thickens and curdles (forms lumps), begin stirring vigorously until the curds disappear and the cheese becomes very thick, smooth and glossy. Keep warm over low heat, stirring occasionally, until ready to use. For a spreadable consistency, remove from the heat and allow the melt to thicken.

Gruyère and Chive Mashed Potatoes
with Peppered Walnuts

Creamy mashed potatoes are blended with melted Gruyère and fresh snipped chives and then garnished with peppery toasted walnuts.

Ingredients:

- 3 pounds Yukon Gold or russet potatoes, peeled and cut into 1-inch chunks
- 1 T olive oil
- 1 cup raw walnut pieces
- sea salt or kosher salt and coarse ground black pepper
- 1 cup Gruyère Melt (pg. 118)
- plain unsweetened non-dairy milk
- 2 T snipped fresh chives

Technique:

Preheat the oven to 350°F. Toss the walnuts in a bowl with the olive oil and a generous amount of pepper. Scatter on a baking sheet and roast for 10 minutes. Remove and set aside.

Place the potatoes in a large pot and cover completely with water. Stir in 2 tsp salt and bring to a boil. Cook the potatoes until tender, about 15 to 20 minutes.

While the potatoes are cooking, prepare the Gruyère Melt. Set aside on low heat to keep warm.

Drain the potatoes and transfer to a large mixing bowl. Mash the potatoes with a potato masher or ricer until crumbly. Add the Gruyère Melt and ¼ cup milk and season with salt and pepper to taste. Whip the potatoes with an electric beater until smooth. Add additional milk as needed until a smooth and creamy but fluffy consistency is achieved. Stir in the snipped chives. Serve immediately and garnish with the peppered walnuts.

French Onion Soup

A classic soup comprised of tender caramelized onions simmered in a rich brown stock, topped with crusty French bread and melted Gruyère and then broiled until the cheese is lightly browned and bubbly. This recipe yields about 6 servings.

Ingredients:

- 6 cups Brown Stock (pg. 121) or commercial vegan "beef" broth
- ¼ cup olive oil
- 3 large sweet yellow onions, peeled and thinly sliced
- 2 tsp organic sugar
- 1 T unbleached all-purpose flour or rice flour
- ¼ cup dry sherry or dry red wine
- 1 bay leaf
- 2 sprigs fresh thyme leaves or ½ tsp dried thyme leaves
- sea salt or kosher salt and coarse ground black pepper, to taste
- 1 French baguette
- 1 cup Gruyère Melt (pg. 118)

Technique:

Add the olive oil to a large cooking pot and place over medium heat. Stir in the sugar. Add the onions and sauté until caramelized.

Sprinkle in the flour, stir until blended and continue to cook until the flour emits a nutty aroma, about 1 minute. Incorporate the stock in increments while stirring and bring to a boil. Stir in the dry sherry or wine and add the bay leaf and thyme.

Reduce the heat to a gentle simmer, partially cover the pot and cook for 30 minutes, stirring occasionally. Season the soup with salt and pepper to taste.

Preheat the oven to 325°F.

While the soup is simmering, prepare the Gruyère Melt. After preparation, remove from the heat to allow the melt to thicken.

Cut 1-inch thick slices of bread. Place the slices on a baking sheet and toast until lightly browned and crisp, about 10 minutes. Remove from the oven.

Set the oven on "Broil".

Remove the bay leaf and ladle the soup into oven-safe soup bowls. Spread a generous amount of the Gruyère melt on each bread slice and top each soup bowl. Place the soup bowls on the baking sheet for easier handling.

Place under the broiler until the cheese is lightly browned and bubbly. Serve immediately.

Brown Stock

This basic stock has a rich brown color and a savory flavor. It can be used as a base for preparing 'au jus', demi-glace, brown gravies and a variety of hearty soups and stews, such as French Onion Soup (pg. 120). This recipe yields 8 cups of prepared stock.

Ingredients:

- 8 cups water
- outer layers from 1 large onion
- peelings from 1 large carrot or 1 T dehydrated carrot flakes
- 6 parsley stems
- 3 cloves garlic, crushed
- ½ cup tamari, soy sauce or Bragg Liquid Aminos™*
- 4 tsp nutritional yeast flakes
- 2 tsp dark brown sugar
- 2 tsp vegan Worcestershire Sauce
- optional: 1 tsp browning liquid (e.g., Gravy Master™ or Kitchen Bouquet™)

Technique:

Remove the paper skin from the onion and discard. Add the tough, outer layers of the onion to a large cooking pot with the water. Add the carrot peelings (or dehydrated flakes) and additional ingredients. Reserve the peeled carrot and the tender portion of the onion for broth, soups, stews or other recipes.

Bring the stock to a boil. Reduce the heat to low, cover the cooking pot and cook for 30 minutes. Using a slotted spoon, remove the large solids. If using the stock immediately, add vegetables, herbs and spices as desired or as specified in a recipe to create a fully seasoned broth; season with additional salt to taste. For most recipe applications, the stock does not require clarification to remove the small amount of nutritional yeast and seasoning sediment.

If a clear stock is desired, let the liquid cool to room temperature and then pour into a sealable container, discarding any sediment that has settled on the bottom of the cooking pot. Refrigerate for up to 10 days. Any micro-fine particles will settle, further clarifying the stock. Decant the clear portion for use in recipes as needed. The stock can also be stored in the freezer for up to 1 month.

Fondue

Fondue is a Swiss and French dish of melted cheese served in a communal pot (*caquelon*) over a portable stove (*réchaud*) and eaten by dipping long-stemmed forks with bread and/or vegetables into the cheese. The fondue can also be kept warm in a commercial fondue pot or small crock pot.

The cheese fondue mixture should be kept warm enough to keep the fondue smooth and liquid but not so hot that it burns. If this temperature is held until the fondue is finished there will be a thin layer of toasted (not burnt) cheese at the bottom of the fondue pot. This is called *la religieuse* (French for "the nun") and is considered a treat.

The fondue was formulated using pure soymilk because of its stability when heated for extended periods; therefore, pure soymilk is recommended for achieving the proper consistency and stability. If you choose to use commercial soymilk with additives or other non-dairy milks, expect variations in results. This recipe yields 1 quart of fondue. For a half portion (2 cups), simply divide the recipe measurements in half.

Ingredients:

- 3 cups pure soymilk
- ½ cup mild vegetable oil
- ½ cup dry sherry or dry white wine
- ½ cup tapioca flour
- ¼ cup nutritional yeast flakes
- ¼ cup mellow white miso paste
- 1 tsp dry ground mustard
- ½ tsp ground coriander
- ¼ tsp ground white pepper
- 2 cloves garlic, crushed, to rub the interior of the fondue or crock pot
- fine sea salt or kosher salt, to taste

Technique:

Rub the interior of the fondue or crock pot with the crushed garlic and discard.

In a large saucepan, vigorously whisk together the fondue ingredients until smooth. Cook the mixture over medium-low heat, stirring slowly and continually with a flexible spatula.

Increase stirring speed as the mixture thickens and begins to form curds. Stir vigorously until the mixture becomes very thick, smooth and glossy. Turn the heat to low to keep the fondue warm while you heat the fondue pot.

Taste the cheese mixture and add salt if needed. If the cheese mixture is too thick, adjust the consistency by adding milk. Transfer the mixture to the heated pot. Serve with chunks of crusty bread and raw or cooked vegetables. Stir the fondue occasionally to prevent the oil from separating and floating to the top of the fondue pot.

Tip: Ask guests to make a figure 8 in the fondue while dipping, as this will ensure that the cheese mixture is frequently stirred.

Non-Dairy Seasoning Blends

Instant "Cheddar" Cheese Sauce Mix

This instant mix is a convenient timesaver for creating a rich and tangy "cheddar" cheese sauce for topping hot sandwiches or pouring over potatoes, pasta, rice or cooked vegetables. This formula yields about 2 cups of dry mix which will make 8 cups of cheddar cheese sauce.

Ingredients:

- 1 cup nutritional yeast flakes
- 1 cup tapioca flour
- 3 T tomato powder
- 3 T onion powder
- 4 tsp fine sea salt or kosher salt
- 2 tsp dry ground mustard
- 2 tsp lactic acid powder
- 1 tsp garlic powder

Technique:

Process the ingredients in a DRY blender or food processor until finely powdered. Store the seasoning blend in an airtight container at room temperature in a cool, dry place for up to 6 months.

To make 1 cup of cheese sauce, whisk together in a small saucepan until smooth:

- ¼ cup dry mix
- ¾ cup plus 2 tablespoons plain unsweetened non-dairy milk (pure soymilk is recommended)
- 2 tablespoons mild vegetable oil

Place the saucepan over medium-low heat and cook the mixture, stirring slowly and continually with a flexible spatula until the mixture becomes thickened, smooth and glossy. Taste and add salt as desired. Reduce the heat to low to keep warm until ready to serve; stir occasionally.

Nacho Cheese No'ritos Seasoning

This zesty cheddar cheese powder was created specifically for dusting pre-salted commercial corn tortilla chips. If frying corn tortillas for chips at home, consider increasing and even doubling the amount of salt in the seasoning recipe. A spicier seasoning can be made by simply adding chipotle chili powder to the blend. Try sprinkling the seasoning on popcorn, French fries or baked potatoes too for a tangy, "South of the Border" nacho cheddar cheese flavor. This recipe yields about 1 cup of seasoning.

Ingredients:

- 1 cup nutritional yeast flakes
- 3 T onion powder
- 3 T tomato powder
- 4 tsp fine sea salt or kosher salt, or more to taste
- 4 tsp mild chili powder (or any ratio of mild chili powder and chipotle chili powder)
- 2 tsp green bell pepper powder
- 2 tsp lactic acid powder
- 1 tsp garlic powder
- 1 tsp dry ground mustard

Technique:

Process the ingredients in a DRY blender until finely powdered. Store the seasoning blend in an airtight container at room temperature in a cool, dry place for up to 6 months (but you'll never keep it around that long!)

To season a large bag of commercial tortilla chips, open the bag and add about 3 tablespoons of seasoning. Close the bag tightly and gently shake and turn to distribute the seasoning. Open the bag and enjoy.

Alternately, add the seasoning powder to a shaker dispenser and season your favorite foods and snacks according to taste.

Cool Buttermilk Ranch No'ritos Seasoning

This cool and creamy buttermilk ranch seasoning powder was created specifically for dusting pre-salted corn chips, potato chips and popcorn. For unsalted chips and popcorn, consider increasing and even doubling the amount of salt in the recipe. This seasoning can also be added to a mixture of Cultured Sour Cream (pg. 37) and No-Eggy Mayo (pg. 140) for an instant ranch dip; or added to a mixture of mayo and non-dairy milk for an instant ranch salad dressing. This recipe yields about 1 cup of seasoning.

Ingredients:

- ¾ cup non-GMO instant soymilk powder
  (DO NOT use soy flour or soy protein powder!)
- 2 T onion powder
- 2 T dried parsley flakes
- 1 T fine sea salt or kosher salt, or more to taste
- 2 tsp dried minced chives
- 1 and ½ tsp lactic acid powder
- 1 tsp coarse ground black pepper
- 1 tsp dried dill
- 1 tsp garlic powder
- ½ tsp dry ground mustard

Technique:

Process the ingredients in a DRY blender until the herbs are reduced to small particles but not completely powdered. Store the seasoning blend in an airtight container at room temperature in a cool, dry place for up to 6 months (but you'll never keep it around that long!)

To season a large bag of commercial potato or corn chips, open the bag and add 2 to 3 tablespoons of seasoning. Close the bag tightly and gently shake and turn to distribute the seasoning. Open the bag and enjoy. Alternately, add the seasoning powder to a shaker dispenser and season your favorite foods and snacks according to taste.

Eggless Egg Specialties

Sunrise Scramble

I'm always looking for ways to improve the texture of certain plant-based foods and the basic tofu scramble has been one of them. When scrambled eggs are made with real eggs, the spatula scrapes the beaten egg mixture into curds as the eggs cook and begin to set, thus creating the scrambled texture. So rather than crumbling the tofu (which always resembles crumbled tofu rather than scrambled eggs), the tofu is sliced into thin "sheets" before cooking. This takes a couple more minutes than crumbling, but the finished texture is remarkable. The other secret to a velvety scramble is to avoid pressing all the water out of the tofu. You'll want to press the excess water, but some water is essential for a velvety texture.

After cooking, try folding in some shredded non-dairy cheese that melts before serving; or top with sautéed vegetables; or slices of fresh avocado and salsa. For a classic American breakfast, serve with hash browns, vegan bacon or sausages and whole grain toast with non-dairy butter. This recipe yields 2 to 4 servings.

Ingredients:

- 2 and ½ tsp Sunrise Scramble Seasoning Blend (recipe follows); or
  - 2 tsp nutritional yeast flakes
  - ½ tsp onion powder
  - ½ tsp kala namak (Himalayan black salt)
  - ¼ tsp sweet paprika
  - ¼ tsp turmeric
- 1 block (14 oz.) soft to firm water-packed tofu*
- 2 T Better Butter (pg. 28) or Vital Butter (pg. 33)
- 2 T pure soymilk
- sea salt or kosher salt and coarse ground black pepper, to taste

Technique:

Measure the scramble seasoning into a small dish and set aside.

Drain and press the tofu on paper towels to remove excess water, but don't press dry. Place the block of tofu on a work surface and with a knife, slice or scrape thin sheets from the narrow side of the block. Use a light touch and glide the knife through the surface of the tofu. Uniform sheets are unnecessary and imperfection will look more natural.

Melt the butter in a non-stick skillet over medium-low heat. Avoid browning the butter. Whisk in the milk and the seasonings and stir until smooth. Increase the heat to medium and continue to stir until the "yolk" mixture thickens slightly.

Add the thinly sliced sheets of tofu and "scramble" (push, lift and fold the mixture with a spatula; don't mash) until the tofu is evenly coated with the seasoning mixture. It will take a minute or two for the tofu to begin absorbing the color from the "yolk" mixture. Pushing and folding will usually break up solid sheets into natural looking "curds" but use the edge of the spatula if necessary. Cook until the mixture is heated through, the color is evenly dispersed and the tofu resembles scrambled eggs. Season the scramble with salt and pepper to taste (keep in mind that the scramble already contains salt). Serve immediately.

Sunrise Scramble Seasoning Blend

When preparing tofu scrambles, achieving the ideal balance of color and flavor can often be tricky. This blend will alleviate the guesswork for you; and if you prepare scrambles frequently, then this seasoning blend will be a timesaver in your morning breakfast routine. This recipe will season 8 Sunrise Scrambles (see previous recipe). For preparing your own scramble recipes, use 2 and ½ tsp seasoning powder for each block of tofu.

Ingredients:

- ⅓ cup nutritional yeast flakes
- 4 tsp onion powder
- 4 tsp kala namak (Himalayan black salt)
- 2 tsp sweet paprika
- 2 tsp turmeric

Technique:

Place the ingredients in a **dry** mini-blender and process into a fine powder. Store the seasoning blend in an airtight container in your pantry until ready to use. Use the powder within 6 months.

Sunnyside-Ups

Delicate slices of silken tofu are lightly seasoned with kala namak (Himalayan black salt), gently pan-seared and then topped with no-yolks sauce. This rich sauce remarkably simulates egg yolk and is wonderful for dipping toast, bacun and sausage.

Ingredients:

- 1 carton (12.3 oz.) Mori-Nu™ extra-firm silken tofu, or similar
- kala namak (Himalayan black salt)
- cooking oil spray
- No-Yolks Sauce (pg. 129)

Technique:

Cut open one end of the carton of silken tofu, drain the water and gently slide out the tofu. Handle it carefully as it is very delicate and will break easily. Transfer the tofu to a work surface, turn the block on its side and slice lengthwise to create 4 even slabs. Place the slabs on a plate lined with several layers of paper towels or a lint-free kitchen towel to drain for a minimum of 20 minutes. If desired, cut each slab into a round using a 3-inch ring mold or biscuit cutter. Discard the remnants or save for another recipe.

Place a small amount of kala namak into a small dish and with a water-moistened fingertip carefully rub some of the salt over the tofu slices. Set aside.

Prepare the no-yolks sauce and keep warm over low heat, stirring occasionally.

Mist a non-stick skillet with cooking oil spray and place over medium heat. When the skillet is hot, add the tofu slices and pan-sear until lightly golden on both sides. Transfer to a serving plate and spoon a generous teaspoon of the sauce onto the center of each slice. Pour additional sauce into individual serving cups on each plate for dipping.

No-Yolks Sauce

No-yolks sauce is a rich dipping sauce that remarkably simulates lightly-cooked liquid egg yolk. This recipe yields about 1 cup of sauce. The recipe can be doubled if desired and stored in the refrigerator for up to 7 days and reheated at your convenience.

Ingredients:

- 1 T nutritional yeast flakes
- ¼ tsp guar gum, sodium alginate or xanthan gum*
- ¼ tsp kala namak (Himalayan black salt), or more to taste
- ⅛ tsp sweet paprika
- ⅛ tsp turmeric
- ½ cup water
- ¼ cup pure soymilk
- ¼ cup Better Butter (pg. 28) or Vital Butter (pg. 33)**

*Guar gum, sodium alginate and xanthan gum are food gums. Gums are superior to food starch for creating the authentic "yolk" texture, mouth feel and stable consistency of this sauce. Food gum can be replaced with 2 teaspoons of food starch if necessary; however the texture, mouth feel and stability of the sauce will differ.

**Do not substitute with oil. The lecithin in non-dairy butter is essential to emulsification of the sauce.

Technique:

In a small dish, combine the nutritional yeast, gum or alginate, kala namak, paprika and turmeric. Combine the water and soymilk together in a cup.

In a small saucepan, melt the butter over low heat. Before the butter begins to brown, whisk in the seasoning blend and stir until smooth.

Whisk in the water and soymilk in increments. Increase the heat to medium-low and cook, stirring frequently until the sauce comes to a simmer. The egg "yolk" color will develop as the mixture heats. Reduce the heat to low and occasionally give the sauce a gentle stir until ready to serve.

Note: Initially the sauce may seem a bit thin, but it will thicken to the ideal texture as it stands. Liquids thickened with food gums are subject to "shear thinning". This means that stirring or shaking will thin the liquid, yet the liquid will thicken after stirring or shaking stops.

Over-Easys

Delicately seasoned and crumbled silken tofu is lightly "scrambled" and served over whole grain English muffins or toast with a generous drizzle of no-yolks sauce. This dish is reminiscent of soft-boiled eggs served over toast.

Ingredients:

- 1 carton (12.3 oz.) Mori-Nu™ extra-firm silken tofu, or similar
- ½ tsp kala namak (Himalayan black salt)
- cooking oil spray
- No-Yolks Sauce (pg. 129)
- 2 whole grain English Muffins or 2 slices of bread cut on the diagonal
- Better Butter (pg. 28) or Vital Butter (pg. 33), for buttering the toast or English muffins

Technique:

Remove the tofu from the carton. Slice the tofu into 4 slabs and place the slabs on a plate lined with several layers of paper towels or a lint-free kitchen towel to drain for a minimum of 20 minutes. Firmly blot the tofu with additional towels to remove as much moisture as possible. This step is very important to ensure the proper texture.

Prepare the no-yolks sauce and keep warm over low heat, stirring occasionally.

Mist a non-stick skillet with cooking oil spray and place over medium heat. While the skillet is heating, toast the English muffins or bread slices.

When the skillet is hot, crumble the silken tofu into the skillet. Season with ¼ teaspoon of kala namak and gently "scramble" the tofu until heated through. Remove from the heat. Butter the English muffins or toast and place on serving plates. Top with the scrambled silken tofu and generously drizzle with the no-yolks sauce. Garnish with black pepper and serve immediately.

No-No Huevos Rancheros

No-No Huevos Rancheros is my variation of Huevos Rancheros (Spanish for "rancher's eggs"). The basic dish consists of layers of refried beans, homemade chunky salsa and lightly fried corn tortillas. The layers are topped with pan-seared silken tofu with No-Yolks sauce and garnished with sliced avocado and cilantro. Spanish rice is a suggested accompaniment.

There are several components to this dish but it's really very easy to assemble once the components are constructed and the results are well worth the effort. This recipe yields 4 servings.

Ingredients:

- 1 carton (12.3 oz.) Mori-Nu™ extra-firm silken tofu, or similar
- 1 can (16 oz.) vegetarian or fat-free refried beans
- kala namak (Himalayan black salt)
- cooking oil spray
- 8 corn tortillas
- sliced avocado
- chopped cilantro for garnish, optional
- No-Yolks Sauce (pg. 129)

Salsa ingredients:

- olive oil
- ½ medium onion, chopped (about ½ cup)
- 1 can (15 oz.) diced tomatoes, preferably fire-roasted
  or 2 large vine-ripened tomatoes, when in season*
- 1 can (4 oz.) diced mild green chilies
- 3 cloves garlic, minced
- 1 tsp ancho chili powder
  (or ½ tsp ancho and ½ tsp chipotle for a spicier sauce)
- ½ tsp ground cumin
- sea salt or kosher salt, to taste

*Blanch fresh tomatoes in boiling water for 1 minute and then plunge in an ice water bath to ease removal of the skins before dicing.

Technique:

Cut open one end of the carton of silken tofu, drain the water and gently slide out the tofu. Handle it carefully as it is very delicate and will break easily. Transfer the tofu to a work surface, turn the block on its side and slice lengthwise to create 4 even slabs. Place the slabs on a plate lined with several layers of paper towels or a lint-free kitchen towel to drain for a minimum of 20 minutes. If desired, cut each slab into a round using a 3-inch ring mold or biscuit cutter. Discard the remnants or save for another recipe.

Place a small amount of kala namak into a small dish and with a water-moistened fingertip carefully rub some of the salt over the tofu slices. Set aside.

Next, prepare the salsa (for convenience, this can be done ahead of time, refrigerated and re-warmed prior to serving). Commercial chunky salsa can be substituted, if desired.

To prepare the salsa, sauté the onions in 2 tablespoons of olive oil in a medium size skillet over medium heat. Once translucent, add the tomatoes and any juice from the tomatoes. If you are using fresh tomatoes, chop them first, then add. Please note that fresh tomatoes will take longer to cook than canned tomatoes, since canned tomatoes are already partially cooked during the canning process. Add the chopped green chilies and the seasonings. Bring to a simmer, reduce heat to low, and let simmer while you prepare the rest of the dish, stirring occasionally. Reduce heat to warm after the salsa has been simmering for 10 minutes (20 minutes for fresh tomatoes); add salt to taste.

Next, warm the refried beans in a covered saucepan over low heat. Add a little water as necessary to thin to a slightly saucy consistency.

Prepare the no-yolks sauce and keep warm over low heat, stirring occasionally.

Now prepare the tortillas. Heat the oven to its lowest setting and place serving plates in the oven to keep warm. Heat a tablespoon of olive oil in a large non-stick or well-seasoned cast iron skillet on medium high, coating the pan with the oil. One by one, heat the tortillas in the skillet for a minute or two on each side until they are heated through and softened (add additional oil as necessary). Stack them on one of the warming plates in the oven to keep warm.

Add another tablespoon of olive oil to the skillet and place over medium heat. When the skillet is hot, add the tofu slices and pan-sear until lightly golden on both sides.

To serve, spoon some of the salsa onto a warmed plate. Top with a tortilla, some refried beans and another tortilla. Place the tofu on top of the tortilla. Place a spoonful of no-yolks sauce in the center of the tofu and spoon the additional salsa around the tofu. Garnish with avocado slices and optional cilantro.

Eggless Eggs Mornay

Delicate slices of silken tofu are lightly seasoned with kala namak (Himalayan black salt), gently pan-seared and then layered over whole grain toast or English Muffins with a rich Mornay sauce. The dish is broiled until the cheese sauce is bubbly and lightly browned and garnished with paprika and parsley. Serves 2 to 4.

Ingredients:

- 1 carton (12.3 oz.) Mori-Nu™ extra-firm silken tofu, or similar
- kala namak (Himalayan black salt)
- cooking oil spray
- Mornay Sauce (pg. 106)
- 2 slices whole grain bread or 2 English muffins, split
- sweet paprika
- chopped parsley

Technique:

Cut open one end of the carton of silken tofu, drain the water and gently slide out the tofu. Handle it carefully as it is very delicate and will break easily. Transfer the tofu to a work surface, turn the block on its side and slice lengthwise to create 4 even slabs. Place the slabs on a plate lined with several layers of paper towels or a lint-free kitchen towel to drain for a minimum of 20 minutes. If desired, cut each slab into a round using a 3-inch ring mold or biscuit cutter. Discard the remnants or save for another recipe.

Place a small amount of kala namak into a small dish and with a water-moistened fingertip carefully rub some of the salt over the tofu slices. Set aside.

Prepare the Mornay sauce and keep warm over low heat, stirring occasionally.

Mist a non-stick skillet with cooking oil spray and place over medium heat. When the skillet is hot, add the tofu slices and pan-sear until lightly golden on both sides. While the tofu is cooking, toast the bread or English muffins.

Set the oven on "Broil". If using toast, cut the slices on a diagonal. Place the toast diagonals or English muffin halves in a shallow baking dish. Top with the tofu slices and then generously cover with the Mornay sauce. Broil until the sauce is lightly browned and bubbly, about 2 minutes. Garnish with paprika and parsley and serve immediately.

Eggless Omelets

Light and delicate eggless omelets can be filled with your choice of ingredients. The cooking technique is very important with this recipe, so follow the directions carefully to ensure success. It is essential to use a non-stick skillet to prevent the omelets from sticking. This recipe yields 2 omelets.

Ingredients:

- 1 carton (12.3 oz.) Mori-Nu™ extra-firm silken tofu, or similar
- 3 T cornstarch, unmodified potato starch or arrowroot flour
- 1 T Better Butter (pg. 28) or Vital Butter (pg. 33), softened; plus additional for "greasing" the skillet
- 1 tsp nutritional yeast flakes
- ½ tsp onion powder
- ½ tsp kala namak (Himalayan black salt)
- ⅛ tsp sweet paprika
- ⅛ tsp turmeric
- fillings and toppings of your choice

Tip: Cheese Melts work beautifully for omelets since the cheese is already melted. See page 110.

Technique:

Remove the tofu from the carton. Slice the tofu into 4 slabs and place the slabs on a plate lined with several layers of paper towels or a lint-free kitchen towel to drain for a minimum of 20 minutes. Firmly blot the tofu with additional towels to remove as much moisture as possible. This step is very important or the omelets will not set properly.

Crumble the tofu into a food processor and add the starch, nutritional yeast flakes, butter, onion powder, kala namak, paprika and turmeric. Process the contents until smooth. The ingredients will form a thick, pale cream (the egg color will develop when the mixture is cooked). Transfer the mixture to a bowl and set aside while any fillings are prepared.

When using vegetables that have high moisture content, such as mushrooms, spinach, zucchini, diced tomatoes, etc., be sure to sauté them until they have released most of their liquid and are cooked through. Transfer the vegetables and other fillings to a separate bowl and set aside.

In the same non-stick skillet over medium heat, melt 1 to 2 tablespoons of butter. Add half of the omelet mixture (¾ cup) to the center of the skillet. Mist the back of large spoon or flexible spatula with cooking oil spray and use it to lightly and gently spread or "fan" the mixture from the center of the skillet outwards towards the edge, spreading as evenly as possible. Admittedly, this can be a little tricky as the omelet mixture is thick and will have a tendency to slide around in the skillet. Just do the best you can. DO NOT add water to thin the consistency of the omelet mixture or the omelets will not set properly!

Reduce the heat to just above low and cover the skillet with a lid. It doesn't matter if the lid was made for the skillet, or if it fits correctly, as long as the skillet can be covered to hold in steam while the omelet mixture cooks. Let the mixture cook undisturbed, about 5 minutes. DO NOT STIR! The goal is to slow cook the omelet (the steam generated will help cook the surface).

Lift the lid to check the omelet. If the surface still appears wet, replace the lid and continue to cook until the surface is dry. This may take several minutes, so do not rush this step. Test the surface of the omelet with your finger, if it feels dry and somewhat firm to the touch, place the filling on one side of the omelet. With a wide spatula, carefully lift the opposite side of the omelet over the filling. Replace the lid and cook an additional 30 seconds to 1 minute to give the cheese a chance to melt.

Slide the omelet onto a serving plate and place in a warm oven while repeating the procedure with the second omelet. Be sure to melt additional butter in the skillet before adding the remaining omelet mixture. If desired, garnish the omelets with a dollop of non-dairy sour cream, salsa or other toppings of choice.

Eggless Frittata

A frittata is essentially an open-faced omelet. Traditionally it is cooked on the stove and then placed under a broiler to set the top. However, my version is baked, which makes it a breeze to cook since it cooks both sides at the same time. The frittata can be baked in a 9-inch oven-safe stainless steel skillet or aluminum pie plate. Chock full of colorful vegetables, the frittata makes a nice breakfast or brunch dish for 2.

Ingredients:

- 1 carton (12.3 oz.) Mori-Nu™ extra-firm silken tofu, or similar
- 3 T cornstarch, unmodified potato starch, or arrowroot powder
- 1 T Better Butter (pg. 28) or Vital Butter (pg. 33), softened
- 1 tsp nutritional yeast flakes
- ½ tsp onion powder
- ¼ tsp kala namak (Himalayan black salt)
- ¼ tsp coarse ground black pepper, or more to taste
- ⅛ tsp sweet paprika
- ⅛ tsp turmeric (a pinch)
- 2 cups finely chopped or shredded vegetables of choice
- 2 T olive oil, plus extra for "greasing" the skillet
- ½ tsp dried thyme
- optional: ½ cup shredded Block and Wheel Cheese of your choice

Technique:

Remove the tofu from the carton. Slice the tofu into 4 slabs and place the slabs on a plate lined with several layers of paper towels or a lint-free kitchen towel to drain for a minimum of 20 minutes. Firmly blot the tofu with additional towels to remove as much moisture as possible. This step is very important or the frittata will not set properly.

Crumble the tofu into a food processor; add the starch, softened butter, nutritional yeast flakes, onion powder, kala namak, paprika and turmeric and process until smooth. The ingredients will form a thick, pale cream. Please note that the egg color will develop when the mixture is cooked. Transfer the mixture to a bowl and set aside while the vegetables are prepared.

Preheat the oven to 375°F. Generously grease a nine-inch oven-safe skillet (or pie plate) with butter and set aside.

Heat the olive oil in a separate skillet over medium heat and sauté the vegetables until cooked through. This is especially important if using vegetables with high moisture content (mushrooms and zucchini, for example). Transfer the vegetables to the bowl with the tofu mixture, add the thyme and stir thoroughly to combine. Spoon the mixture into the skillet (or pie plate) and smooth the top with the spatula or back of a spoon. Top with the optional shredded cheese, if desired.

Bake for 35 minutes. Remove from the heat and let cool for about 10 minutes before slicing and serving. The frittata should be fairly easy to remove from the skillet and placed on a serving plate, if desired. Simply slide a flat spatula underneath to loosen and remove.

Mushroom, Onion and Suisse Quiche

Mushroom, Onion and Suisse Quiche is an open-faced pastry crust pie filled with a blend of silken tofu custard, shredded Suisse cheese and sautéed mushrooms and onions. Any combination of other vegetables or plant-based meats can be substituted, as well as any of the firm Block and Wheel Cheeses in this book.

Ingredients:

- 2 cartons (12.3 oz. each) Mori-Nu™ extra-firm silken tofu, or similar
- 1 basic pastry crust (9")
- 2 T olive oil
- ½ cup diced onion
- 6 oz. mushrooms, any variety, thinly sliced
- 5 T unmodified potato starch, cornstarch or arrowroot powder
- 2 tsp nutritional yeast flakes
- ¾ tsp kala namak (Himalayan black salt)
- ½ dried thyme
- ½ tsp coarse ground black pepper
- 1 cup shredded Suisse cheese (pg. 73)

Notes: The mushrooms and onions can be replaced with any combination of vegetables or plant-based meats; however, avoid exceeding 10 ounces total (before cooking). It is essential to cook the ingredients thoroughly to remove as much moisture as possible in order for the quiche to set properly.

Technique:

Drain the tofu and slice each block into 4 slabs. Place the slabs on a plate lined with several layers of paper towels or a lint-free kitchen towel to drain for a minimum of 20 minutes. After 20 minutes, blot the surface of the tofu with additional towels to remove as much moisture as possible. This step is very important or the quiche will fail to set properly.

Prepare and pre-bake the pastry crust for 12 minutes at 375°F. Remove and let cool but leave the oven on.

Add the olive oil to a skillet and sauté the onions and mushrooms over medium heat until the mushrooms have completely released their moisture and the onions are beginning to caramelize. It is essential that the mixture be cooked thoroughly. Stir in the thyme and black pepper and set aside to cool.

Crumble the silken tofu into a food processor. Add the starch, yeast and kala namak. Process the contents until smooth. Transfer the tofu mixture to a mixing bowl. Stir in the sautéed mushrooms, onions and the shredded cheese. Mix thoroughly.

Spoon the filling into the pastry crust and smooth the surface with the back of the spoon. Bake uncovered for 50 minutes. Let the quiche cool for about 15 to 20 minutes to allow it to "set" before slicing and serving. If the quiche needs to be reheated, cover securely with foil and heat in the oven at 350°F for 10 to 15 minutes; or cover with plastic wrap and reheat in the microwave.

Bedeviled Eggless Eggs

Bedeviled eggless eggs are remarkably similar to deviled eggs in appearance, taste and texture. They make the perfect bite-size finger food for vegan BBQs, picnics and parties. Kala namak, or Himalayan black salt, is essential to impart that familiar egg-like taste to these savory bites. This recipe yields 16 to 24 bedeviled eggless eggs.

A blender is required for preparing the "egg whites" and a food processor is recommended for the "yolk filling". You will also need an 8" square baking pan and 1 block (14 oz.) of extra-firm water-packed tofu. Drain and press the tofu until it is not releasing any more liquid - this is very important! After pressing you will have approximately 12 oz. of tofu.

Ingredients for the "egg whites":

- ⅓ block (about 4 oz.) extra-firm water-packed tofu, pressed
- ¾ tsp kala namak (Himalayan black salt)
- 2 cups water
- 2 and ½ tsp agar powder

Ingredients for the "yolk" filling:

- ⅔ block (about 8 oz.) extra-firm water-packed tofu, pressed
- 3 T No-Eggy Mayo (pg. 140)
- 1 T nutritional yeast flakes
- 1 T dill pickle brine
- 2 tsp Dijon mustard or spicy golden mustard
- ½ tsp onion powder
- ¼ tsp kala namak* (Himalayan black salt), or more to taste
- ¼ tsp turmeric
- ¼ tsp paprika (for extra bedeviling, use cayenne pepper)

Garnishes:

- paprika and coarse ground black pepper
- optional: sliced black olives; fresh snipped chives; capers or chopped dill

Technique:

To prepare the "egg whites", place the "egg white" ingredients into a blender and process until smooth. Pour the mixture into a saucepan and bring to rapid simmer over medium heat, stirring frequently to avoid scorching the tofu mixture. Pour the mixture into the 8" baking pan and set aside to cool.

Tip: If you have chocolate egg molds, or a heat-proof container that specifically holds deviled eggs, the tofu mixture can be poured into the molds to create perfect, halved hard-boiled egg shapes.

Next, crumble the ⅔ block of pressed tofu into the food processor and add the remaining "yolk" filling ingredients. Process the contents until completely smooth, stopping as necessary to scrape down the sides of the food processor. Alternately, the mixture can be mashed using a fork or a potato masher/ricer, but the mixture will not be as smooth.

Transfer the "yolk" mixture to a bowl or food storage container, season with additional kala namak if desired, cover and refrigerate until ready to use. Cover the baking pan with plastic wrap or foil and refrigerate until the "egg whites" have completely set, or a minimum of 30 minutes.

Now, run a table knife around the perimeter of the baking pan to loosen the "egg white" (or simply pop them out of the chocolate egg molds). Invert the baking pan onto a clean work surface. At this point, the "egg white" can be cut into rectangles or cut into rounds or ovals.

For rectangles, cut the "egg whites" into 6 even strips. Turn your cutting surface and make 4 even slices. This will create 24 rectangles. For rounds or ovals, use a 1 and ½-inch to 1 and ¾-inch cookie cutter or ring mold. Any "egg white" remnants can be finely diced and mixed with any of the leftover "yolk" filling for a quick eggless egg salad sandwich.

Spoon a generous teaspoonful of the "yolk" mixture onto the top of each "egg white". Alternately, the mixture can be decoratively piped onto the "egg whites" using a pastry bag. If you don't have a pastry bag, try placing the mixture into a zip-lock bag, seal and then snip off a tiny piece from the bottom corner of the bag with scissors. Squeeze the bag to pipe the mixture onto the "egg whites".

Sprinkle with paprika and garnish with optional ingredients as desired. Cover gently with plastic wrap and chill thoroughly before serving.

Eggless Egg Salad

This tasty sandwich filling remarkably resembles real egg salad in appearance taste and texture, but without the cholesterol (or animal cruelty). A blender is required for preparing the "egg whites" and a food processor is recommended for the "yolk" mixture. You will also need 1 block (14 oz.) of extra-firm water-packed tofu. Drain and press the tofu until it is not releasing any more liquid - this is very important! After pressing you will have approximately 12 oz. of tofu.

Ingredients for the "egg whites":

- ⅓ block (about 4 oz.) extra-firm water-packed tofu, pressed
- ¾ tsp kala namak (Himalayan black salt)
- 2 cups water
- 2 and ½ tsp agar powder

Ingredients for the "yolk" mixture:

- ⅔ block (about 8 oz.) extra-firm water-packed tofu, pressed
- ¼ cup No-Eggy Mayo (pg. 140), plus additional as necessary for consistency
- 1 T nutritional yeast flakes
- 2 tsp prepared mustard, your choice of Dijon, spicy, golden or yellow
- ¼ tsp kala namak (Himalayan black salt), or more to taste
- ¼ tsp turmeric
- ¼ tsp paprika
- 2 T minced onion
- 1 rib of celery, diced
- coarse ground black pepper to taste
- optional ingredients: sliced black olives, capers, or diced pickle

Technique:

To prepare the "egg whites", place the "egg white" ingredients into a blender and process until smooth. Pour the mixture into a saucepan and bring to rapid simmer over medium heat, stirring frequently to avoid scorching the tofu mixture. Pour the mixture into any food storage container and set aside to cool.

Next, crumble the ⅔ pressed block of pressed tofu into a food processor and add the mayo, nutritional yeast flakes, prepared mustard, kala namak, turmeric and paprika. Process the contents until completely smooth, stopping as necessary to scrape down the sides of the food processor. Alternately, the mixture can be mashed using a fork but the mixture will not be as smooth.

Transfer the "yolk" mixture to a bowl or a food storage container and stir in the minced onion, celery, black pepper and any optional ingredients. Mix well, cover and refrigerate until ready to use. Cover the "egg white" container and refrigerate until the "egg whites" have completely set, or a minimum of 30 minutes.

Now, run a table knife around the perimeter of the "egg white" container to loosen if necessary and invert onto a work surface. Chop the "egg whites" into fine dice and transfer to a mixing bowl. Stir in the "yolk" mixture and add additional mayonnaise as necessary to thoroughly moisten the eggless salad. Season the mixture with additional salt and pepper as desired, cover with plastic wrap and chill thoroughly before serving.

No-Eggy Mayo

This recipe produces an eggless mayonnaise that rivals real egg mayonnaise in both taste and texture and is much less expensive than commercial dairy/egg-free mayonnaise. The ingredients are readily available in most markets and an immersion blender or food processor makes this a nearly foolproof method for making mayonnaise.

The advantage of using a food processor is that the machine does most of the work for you. The advantage of using an immersion blender is that the mayonnaise will be thicker, yet requires less oil. The disadvantage of the immersion blender is that your hand and arm may become tired from controlling the blender. The immersion blender method also requires a little dexterity to manage blending with one hand and pouring the oil with the other hand. If another person can help pour the oil, the process is much easier.

I have personally used both methods many, many times and now favor the immersion blender method for producing the best quality mayonnaise. It's definitely more of a chore, but the results are well worth it. A standard or high-powered blender is not recommended for making mayonnaise because once the mixture thickens, it's nearly impossible to keep it turning in the blades while adding the oil.

Sunflower, safflower, canola and soybean oil are the best oils for making this mayonnaise. Extra-virgin or virgin olive oil will add a bitter undertaste to the mayonnaise. If you wish to include olive oil, reduce the carrier oil by ½ cup and mix ½ cup olive oil into the carrier oil.

This is my own signature blend and yields about 2 cups of the finest egg-free mayonnaise.

Ingredients:

- ½ cup pure soymilk, chilled
  (sorry, no substitutions; other plant milks will not emulsify properly)
- 1 T plus 1 tsp fresh lemon juice
- 1 tsp apple cider vinegar, preferably raw organic
- 2 tsp organic sugar
- 1 tsp dry ground mustard*
- ¾ to 1 tsp fine sea salt or kosher salt
- pinch of ground white pepper
- pinch of sweet paprika or cayenne pepper
- optional: pinch of kala namak (imparts an egg mayonnaise flavor)
- 1 and ½ cup mild vegetable oil if using an immersion blender; or
  1 and ¾ cup mild vegetable oil if using a food processor

*Do not omit this ingredient! Dry ground mustard not only adds flavor but is a natural emulsifier and therefore essential to the success of this recipe.

Tip: For garlic mayo, add ½ tsp garlic powder, or more to taste, to the soymilk mixture before processing.

Technique:

Measure the oil into a liquid measuring cup (ideally it should have a "lip" for pouring). Set aside.

Immersion blender method:

Place all of the ingredients EXCEPT for the oil into a 4-cup glass measuring cup or heavy glass/ceramic bowl. Insert the immersion blender and process the mixture for about 10 seconds.

Now with the immersion blender running on high speed, SLOWLY drizzle the oil into the blending cup or bowl. Move the blender up and down and side to side as you add the oil (you can stop blending to give your arm a rest as long as you stop pouring the oil; then resume when you're ready). Continue blending until all the oil is incorporated and the mixture is emulsified and very thick. Transfer to a glass jar or plastic container and refrigerate.

Note: I cannot emphasize enough the importance of adding the oil slowly. If you add the oil too fast, the emulsion may break and revert back to a liquid.

Food processor method:

Place all of the ingredients EXCEPT for the oil into a food processor and process the mixture for about 10 seconds.

Turn the food processor on continuous run (if you have speed settings, run on high speed) and SLOWLY begin to drizzle the oil into the mixture through the food chute. The addition of the oil will take about 2 minutes, so be patient and don't rush. You should begin to note a change in the consistency of the mixture after about 1 and ¼ cup of oil has been added. Continue to SLOWLY add the remainder of the oil. As soon as all of the oil has been incorporated, turn the processor off - the mayonnaise is finished. Transfer to a glass jar or plastic container and refrigerate.

Note: I cannot emphasize enough the importance of adding the oil slowly. If you add it too fast, the emulsion may break and revert back to a liquid.

Non-Dairy Sweet Treats

Italian Mascarpone Cheesecake

Italian Mascarpone Cheesecake is deliciously rich and yet very easy-to-make. The Italian mascarpone cheese is created as the cheesecake ingredients are mixed.

Ingredients:

- 1 and ½ cup (7.5 oz) whole raw cashews
- 1 and ¾ cup pure soymilk*
- 1 nine-inch Graham Cracker or Cookie Crumb Pie Shell (recipe follows), or similar
- ¼ cup organic **refined** coconut oil
- ¾ cup organic sugar
- 2 T plus 1 tsp cornstarch, unmodified potato starch or arrowroot powder
- 1 tsp real vanilla extract
- ½ tsp raw apple cider vinegar
- ¼ tsp fine sea salt or kosher salt
- 2 tsp lactic acid powder**

*Soymilk is essential to this recipe since it thickens when combined with the lactic acid; other plant milks will not react in the same manner, so don't use them.

**Lactic acid powder can be replaced with citric acid or ascorbic acid powder; however, these acids will not produce the same lactic dairy flavor.

Technique:

Rinse the cashews to remove any loose dust or debris and drain thoroughly. Add the cashews and the soymilk to a covered container and soak for a minimum of 8 hours in the refrigerator.

When ready to begin, pre-bake the pie shell at 375°F for 12 minutes. Remove from the oven and set aside to cool. Leave the oven on.

While the pie shell is prebaking, remove the lid from the jar of coconut oil and place the jar in a microwave. Heat until the solid oil liquefies, about 30 seconds to 1 minute (this will depend upon the solidity of the coconut oil). Alternately, place the jar in about an inch of simmering water and melt the oil in the same manner. Measure ¼ cup and add to a high-powered blender.

Add the cashews and soymilk to the blender and process the contents on high speed until completely smooth and creamy, stopping to scrape down the sides of the blender jar as necessary. Add the remaining ingredients except for the lactic acid powder and process until blended. Add the lactic acid last and process until blended.

Pour the mixture into the pie crust. Smooth the top with the spatula to release any visible air bubbles. Place in a large, shallow baking dish that will accommodate the 9-inch pie plate.

Slowly pour VERY HOT water into the shallow dish so that the bottom half of the pie plate is submerged (about ½-inch). Avoid overfilling and be careful not to splash water into the cheesecake mixture. The water bath will help the cheesecake to cook more evenly. Being careful not to tip the baking dish, place the dish in the oven and bake for 50 minutes.

Being careful not to tip the baking dish, remove the dish from the oven and set on a level surface to cool. Remove the cheesecake and place on a towel to dry the bottom of the pie plate. When the cheesecake has completely cooled, cover with plastic wrap and refrigerate until completely chilled and firm.

Slice and serve with your favorite fresh fruit, fruit sauce or other toppings as desired.

Graham Cracker or Cookie Crumb Pie Shell

Vegan graham crackers are often difficult to find, so vegan cookie crumbs can always be substituted.

Ingredients:

- 1 and ¾ cup dairy, honey and egg-free graham cracker or cookie crumbs
- 6 T Better Butter (pg. 28) or Vital Butter (pg. 33), melted

Technique:

Mix all ingredients until thoroughly combined. Press firmly onto the bottom and up the sides of a 9-inch pie plate. Cover and refrigerate or freeze until ready to use. The shell requires prebaking for 12 minutes at 375°F before filling.

Variations:

- ❖ For a nutty crust, reduce the crumbs to 1 and ¼ cup and add ½ cup finely ground walnuts, pecans or almonds.
- ❖ For a spiced crust, add 1 tsp ground cinnamon and ½ tsp ground nutmeg.

Chocolate Mascarpone Cheesecake

Ingredients:

- 1 and ½ cup (7.5 oz) whole raw cashews
- 1 and ¾ cup pure soymilk (sorry, no substitutions)*
- 1 nine-inch Graham Cracker or Cookie Crumb Pie Shell (recipe on preceding page), or similar
- ¼ cup organic **refined** coconut oil
- 1 cup organic sugar
- ⅓ cup unsweetened cocoa powder
- 2 T plus 1 tsp cornstarch, unmodified potato starch or arrowroot powder
- 2 tsp real vanilla extract
- ½ tsp raw apple cider vinegar
- ¼ tsp fine sea salt or kosher salt
- 2 tsp lactic acid powder**

*Soymilk is essential to this recipe since it thickens when combined with the lactic acid; other plant milks will not react in the same manner, so don't use them.

**Lactic acid powder can be replaced with citric acid or ascorbic acid powder; however, these acids will not produce the same lactic dairy flavor.

Technique:

Rinse the cashews to remove any loose dust or debris and drain thoroughly. Add the cashews and the soymilk to a covered container and soak for a minimum of 8 hours in the refrigerator.

When ready to begin, pre-bake the pie shell at 375°F for 12 minutes. Remove from the oven and set aside to cool. Leave the oven on.

While the pie shell is prebaking, remove the lid from the jar of coconut oil and place the jar in a microwave. Heat until the solid oil liquefies, about 30 seconds to 1 minute (this will depend upon the solidity of the coconut oil). Alternately, place the jar in about an inch of simmering water and melt the oil in the same manner. Measure ¼ cup and add to a high-powered blender.

Add the cashews and soymilk to the blender and process the contents on high speed until completely smooth and creamy, stopping to scrape down the sides of the blender jar as necessary. Add the remaining ingredients except for the lactic acid powder and process until blended. Add the lactic acid last and process until blended.

Pour the mixture into the pie crust. Smooth the top with the spatula to release any visible air bubbles. Place in a large, shallow baking dish that will accommodate the 9-inch pie plate.

Slowly pour VERY HOT water into the shallow dish so that the bottom half of the pie plate is submerged (about ½-inch). Avoid overfilling and be careful not to splash water into the cheesecake mixture. The water bath will help the cheesecake to cook more evenly. Being careful not to tip the baking dish, place the dish in the oven and bake for 50 minutes.

Being careful not to tip the baking dish, remove the dish from the oven and set on a level surface to cool. Remove the cheesecake and place on a towel to dry the bottom of the pie plate. When the cheesecake has completely cooled, cover with plastic wrap and refrigerate until completely chilled and firm.

Note: The cheesecake will form its own chocolate "glaze" while baking.

Crème Caramel

Crème Caramel, or flan, is a custard dessert with a soft caramel glaze, as opposed to crème brûlée, which is a custard dessert with a hard caramel glaze. It's fairly easy to make and creates a beautiful dessert presentation. This recipe yields six ½-cup servings.

Ingredients for the custard:

- 1 carton (12.3 oz) Mori-Nu™ extra-firm silken tofu, or similar
- 1 can (13.5 oz) organic unsweetened full-fat coconut milk
- ¾ cup organic sugar
- 2 tsp cornstarch or unmodified potato starch
- 1 and ½ tsp agar powder
- 2 tsp real vanilla extract
- ¼ tsp ground cinnamon
- a pinch of freshly grated nutmeg

Ingredients for the caramel glaze:

- ½ cup light brown sugar
- 2 T water
- 2 T Better Butter (pg. 28) or Vital Butter (pg. 33)

Special items needed:

- any shallow, heat-proof, round or square bowl or pan that will hold a minimum of 3 cups liquid

Technique:

Drain the excess liquid from the carton of tofu. Slide out the tofu and place on a layer of paper towels to drain for 15 minutes. Crumble the tofu into a blender, add the remaining custard ingredients and process until smooth. Pour into a medium saucepan and set aside.

To make the caramel, stir together the ½ cup light brown sugar and 2 tablespoons of water in a small saucepan until the sugar is dissolved. Add the butter and bring to a simmer. Reduce the heat to medium-low and continue to cook for exactly 4 minutes. Gently swirl the pan occasionally over the heat but do not stir. Keep warm over low heat until the custard is ready in the next step.

While the caramel mixture is cooking, bring the custard mixture to a simmer over medium heat, stirring frequently. Watch it carefully so it does not boil over. After the mixture has come to a simmer and thickened, remove the pan from the heat source.

Now carefully pour the caramel into the heat-proof custard mold. Tilt the mold in all directions to swirl the caramel evenly across the bottom and partially up the sides.

CAUTION: The sugar mixture is dangerously hot and can cause severe burns. Avoid skin contact at all times!

Now, immediately pour the custard mixture into the mold over the caramel. Let cool at room temperature for about 20 minutes. Cover with plastic wrap and refrigerate for several hours until set.

To remove the custard from the mold, carefully run a knife around the inside perimeter of the mold to loosen the custard. Fill the sink without about ½-inch of very hot water. Set the mold into the sink for few minutes. Wipe the bottom of the mold dry with a towel and place a serving plate on top. Quickly invert the custard onto the plate (you may have to shake the mold to release the custard). Slice and serve.

145

Fresh Fruit Gelato

Gelato is the Italian word for "ice cream" and is derived from the Latin word *gelatus* (meaning frozen). The sugar content in homemade gelato, as in traditional ice cream, is balanced with the cream content to act as an anti-freeze to prevent it from freezing solid. The gelato mixture is typically cooked to dissolve the sugar but the blender works well for this purpose - no cooking required. However, an ice cream maker is required for this recipe.

Ingredients:

- 2 cups Heavy Crēme (pg. 19)
- 1 cup organic sugar
- ½ tsp guar gum, sodium alginate or xanthan gum
- 2 cups chilled fruit purée, smooth or semi-chunky

Technique:

Process the cream, sugar and gum or alginate in a blender (this will dissolve the sugar). Transfer to a sealable container and refrigerate until very cold. When well chilled, pour the cream mixture into your ice cream maker and add the chilled fruit purée. Process the mixture according to your ice cream maker's instructions and then freeze to firm. To serve, thaw briefly until it reaches the desired texture for scooping.

Vanilla Bean (or Chocolate) Gelato

Gelato is the Italian word for "ice cream" and is derived from the Latin word *gelatus* (meaning frozen). The sugar content in homemade gelato, as in traditional ice cream, is balanced with the cream content to act as an anti-freeze to prevent it from freezing solid. An assortment of other ingredients, such as chopped nuts, bits of Marshmallow (pg. 147), bits of dark chocolate, etc. can be added as desired. The gelato mixture is typically cooked to dissolve the sugar but the blender works well for this purpose - no cooking required. However, an ice cream maker is required for this recipe.

Ingredients:

- 4 cups Light Crēme (pg. 19)
- 1 and ¼ cup organic sugar
- 2 tsp real vanilla extract
- caviar (pulp) scraped from 1 split vanilla bean
- ½ tsp guar gum, sodium alginate or xanthan gum

For chocolate ice cream: Omit the vanilla bean and add ⅓ cup unsweetened cocoa or carob powder.

Technique:

Process all ingredients in a blender (this will dissolve the sugar). Transfer to a sealable container and refrigerate until very cold. When well chilled, pour the cream mixture into your ice cream maker. Process the mixture according to your ice cream maker's instructions and then freeze to firm. To serve, thaw briefly until it reaches the desired texture for scooping.

Marshmallows

This is my own recipe for creating firm, puffy, gelatin-free marshmallows. The secret ingredient to this melt-in-your-mouth confection is Versawhip 600K™, which is a modified (enzyme-treated) form of soy protein. Versawhip 600K™ will need to be purchased through the internet and I recommend ModernistPantry.com as the source from which to order. The other essential ingredient is *iota carrageenan*, a seaweed derivative, which can also be purchased through Modernist Pantry. DO NOT use any other form of carrageenan!

A stand mixer with a balloon whisk attachment is REQUIRED for this recipe. The technique involves whipping molten hot sugar syrup, so do not attempt with a hand-held mixer or splattering can occur which can result in severe burns. Food processors, standard or high-powered blenders or immersion blenders are not recommended for this recipe either as they will not work properly. So please don't try it. It is also recommended that the stand mixer be equipped with a splatter shield to prevent the sticky marshmallow mixture from splattering out of the mixing bowl.

You will need a candy thermometer to determine when the molten sugar syrup has reached the proper temperature. Light corn syrup is also required for this recipe. This can be purchased at any grocery store - it is not the same thing as high fructose corn syrup. Non-GMO light corn syrup does exist and is available through the internet (and possibly some health food or natural food stores).

You will also need cooking oil spray for "greasing" the baking pan, and cornstarch, unmodified potato starch or tapioca flour for dusting the pan. A 50/50 mixture of Organic Powdered Sugar (pg. 26) and food starch will be needed for dusting the marshmallows after they have been cut into shapes.

Be sure to read the instructions carefully and thoroughly before beginning to ensure success. This recipe yields one 13"x9" pan of 1" thick marshmallow which can be cut into any shape desired.

Ingredients for the sugar syrup:

- 2 cups organic sugar
- 2 and ½ tsp iota carrageenan
- ¼ tsp fine sea salt
- ½ cup water
- ⅔ cup light corn syrup

Ingredients for the fluff:

- ½ cup water
- 1 T Versawhip 600K™
- ½ tsp guar gum, sodium alginate or xanthan gum
- 1 tsp real vanilla extract

Technique:

Line a 13"x9" baking dish with foil, leaving excess hanging over the sides to create a "sling". Mist the interior with cooking oil spray and then lightly dust with starch. Set aside.

In a small dish, combine the dry Versawhip 600K™ and the guar gum, xanthan gum or alginate. Set aside.

Whisk together the dry sugar, carrageenan and salt in a separate bowl. Dry whisking is very important as the carrageenan needs to be dispersed as evenly as possible. Set aside.

Add ½ cup water to a small saucepan and then add the corn syrup.

Attach a candy thermometer to the side of the saucepan. Be sure the base of the thermometer rests just above the bottom of the pan without touching the metal.

Pour the sugar mixture into the center of the water and corn syrup mixture. Stir the mixture gently with a wire whisk to help dissolve the sugar. Place the saucepan over medium-high heat to bring to a boil. Do not stir the mixture once heating begins. The mixture will need to be heated to the "soft-ball candy" stage or 240°F. This will take several minutes.

While the sugar syrup is boiling, add ½ cup water to the bottom of the mixer's bowl. Sprinkle in the Versawhip 600K™/gum mixture and put the splatter guard in place. Reserve the vanilla extract for later. Turn on the mixer and increase speed to the highest setting. The mixture will whip into a voluminous white foam.

When the sugar syrup has reached 240°F, remove the saucepan from the heat, set the thermometer aside, and with the mixer running at high speed pour the molten sugar syrup into the foam. Avoid contacting the sides of the mixing bowl if possible. Don't worry about scraping the residual syrup sticking to the sides and bottom of the saucepan; it's molten hot and you could potentially burn yourself. Set a timer for 6 minutes while whipping at high speed.

While the mixture is whipping, pour in the vanilla extract.

Lightly spray a sturdy spatula with cooking oil and use it to transfer the marshmallow mixture to the dusted pan. Press to pack and spread the marshmallow into the pan; smooth the surface as best as you can. Re-oil the spatula as necessary to prevent sticking. Loosely cover the pan with plastic wrap and let the marshmallow firm at room temperature for a minimum of 8 hours.

Lift the marshmallow from the pan and place on a work surface. Using an oiled knife or oiled cookie cutter or ring mold, cut the marshmallow into desired shapes.

Place a generous amount of the powdered sugar/starch mixture into a bowl and dust the cut marshmallows on all sides evenly. Shake to remove the excess powder and set the marshmallows into a sealable container. Seal and refrigerate for up to 7 days.

Appendix

U.S. to Metric Liquid and Dry Volume Conversions

¼ teaspoon = 1.23 milliliters

½ teaspoon = 2.46 milliliters

¾ teaspoon = 3.7 milliliters

1 teaspoon = 4.93 milliliters

1 and ¼ teaspoons = 6.16 milliliters

1 and ½ teaspoons = 7.39 milliliters

1 and ¾ teaspoons = 8.63 milliliters

2 teaspoons = 9.86 milliliters

1 tablespoon = 14.79 milliliters

2 tablespoons = 29.57 milliliters

¼ cup = 59.15 milliliters

½ cup = 118.3 milliliters

1 cup = 236.59 milliliters

2 cups or 1 pint = 473.18 milliliters

3 cups = 709.77 milliliters

4 cups or 1 quart = 946.36 milliliters

4 quarts or 1 gallon = 3.785 liters

U.S. to Metric Dry Weight Conversions

1 oz = 28 g

4 oz or ¼ lb = 113 g

8 oz or ½ lb = 230 g

12 oz or ¾ lb = 340 g

1 lb or 16 oz = 450 g

Recipe Index

Almond Milk 17

Americana 80

An Introduction to Non-Dairy Cheeses **42**

An Introduction **1**

An Introduction 54

Appendix - U.S. to Metric Conversions **149**

Baked Manicotti 92

Basil Pesto 87

Bedeviled Eggless Eggs 137

Better Butter 28

Bleu Cheese 52

Block and Wheel Cheeses **54**

Brie (or Camembert) en Croûte with Caramelized Mushrooms and Onions 70

Broccoli Cheddar Soup 78

Brown Stock 121

Buttermilk Ranch Dressing and Dip 35

Cashew Cream 22

Chai Thai Iced Tea 24

Cheese Melts **110**

Cheese Sauces **101**

Cheesy Broccoli, Cauliflower and Rice Casserole 117

Chef's Best Marinara Sauce 93

Chèvre Soja with Basil Pesto and Sun-Dried Tomatoes 86

Chèvre with Fines Herbes 47

Chèvre with Mulled Wine Swirl 48

Chèvre with Rosemary Balsamic Swirl 49

Chèvre 46

Chilled Cucumber Buttermilk Soup 36

Chocolate Cashew Milk and Hot Chocolate 16

Chocolate Mascarpone Cheesecake	144
Chunky Bleu Cheese Dressing	53
Classic Grilled Cheese	116
Classic Mac' and Cheese	102
Colby Melt	110
Cool Buttermilk Ranch No'ritos Seasoning	125
Cottage Cheese	94
Cream Cheese	45
Creamy Ricotta (with optional herbs)	91
Crème Caramel	145
Crēme	19
Cultured Cashew-Based Cheeses	**44**
Cultured Crème Fraîche	38
Cultured Non-Dairy Butter, Buttermilk and Creams	**30**
Cultured Raw Buttermilk	34
Cultured Sour Cream	37
Dill Havarti	72
Eggless Egg Salad	139
Eggless Egg Specialties	**126**
Eggless Eggs Mornay	133
Eggless Frittata	135
Eggless Omelets	134
Eggplant Rollatini	62
Extra-Sharp White Cheddar	51
Fondue	122
French Brie and Camembert	69
French Onion Soup	120
Fresh Fruit Gelato	146
Garlic Herb Gournay	95
Garlic Parmesan Crostini	98

Gloucester with Onions and Chives   82

Golden Cheddar Sauce   101

Golden Cheddar   77

Golden Stock   79

Gorgonzola   88

Gorgonzola, Pear and Candied Walnut Salad   89

Graham Cracker or Cookie Crumb Pie Shell   143

Grated Parmesan   99

Greek Tzatziki   40

Greek-Style Yogurt   38

Gruyère and Chive Mashed Potatoes with Peppered Walnuts   119

Gruyère Melt   118

Hard Parmesan   97

Heavy Whipping Crēme   25

Horchata   18

Iceberg Wedge Salad with Chunky Bleu Cheese Dressing   53

Indian Raita   41

Insalata Mozzarella Fresco   66

Instant Cheddar Cheese Sauce Mix   123

Italian Mascarpone Cheesecake   142

Italian Mascarpone   100

Jarlsberg Melt   112

Käsespätzle (German Spätzle with Cheese and Onions)   113

Mango Lassi   41

Marshmallows   147

Mediterranean Herbed Feta   85

Miscellaneous Cheeses   **97**

Mornay Sauce   106

Mozzarella di Campana   64

Mozzarella di Tuscano   63

Mozzarella Fior di Latte	60
Mozzarella Fresco	65
Muenster	74
Mushroom, Onion and Suisse Quiche	136
Nacho Cheese No'ritos Seasoning	124
No-Eggy Mayo	140
Non-Dairy Butter	**28**
Non-Dairy Creams	**19**
Non-Dairy Milks	**12**
Non-Dairy Seasoning Blends	**123**
Non-Dairy Sweet Treats	**142**
No-No Huevos Rancheros	131
No-Yolks Sauce	129
Organic Powdered Sugar	26
Over-Easys	130
Pepper Jack	71
Peppercorn Chèvre	47
Pizza Margherita	67
Potato Cheese Soup	81
Potatoes Dauphinoise	105
Preparation and Cooking Technique	57
Provolone Affumicata (Smoked Provolone)	68
Queso Blanco Sauce	108
Queso Fresco	90
Queso Nacho Sauce	107
Quick Buttermilk	13
Quick Crème Fraîche	20
Raw Cashew Milk	15
Recipe Index	**150**
Rejuvelac	30

Rice Milk   18

Risotto Parmesan   98

Saganaki   61

Salsa con Queso   109

Sauce Fromage Blanc   104

Scalloped Potatoes Gratin   103

Seasoned Butter   29

Sharp Tofu Cheddar   83

Smoked Gouda   75

Smoked Gouda, Spinach and Artichoke Dip   76

Soymilk   12

Spätzle   114

Spinach Ricotta   91

Suisse   73

Sunnyside-Ups   128

Sunrise Scramble Seasoning Blend   127

Sunrise Scramble   126

Sweetened Coffee Creamer #1   21

Sweetened Coffee Creamer #2   23

Tangy Cheddar Melt   115

The Non-Dairy Glossary   **2**

Tofu-Based Cheeses   **83**

Troubleshooting Tips   59

Twice-Baked Cheesy Broccoli Potatoes   111

Vanilla Bean (or Chocolate) Gelato   146

Vital Butter   33

Whipped Coconut Cream   27

White Cheddar Amandine   50

Whole Soymilk and Chocolate Soymilk   14

Zesty Onion Dill Gournay   96